Smear

Knowing an~~~~~~~~~~ the Narcissist's Campaign

By

HG Tudor

Smeared:

Knowing and Beating the Narcissist's Campaign

By

H G Tudor

Published by Insight Books

Introduction

If you have been involved with a narcissist there is a good chance that you will have been subjected to a smear campaign. The smear campaign is the deliberate blackening of the character and reputation of the target in the eyes of one or more people. A smear campaign may operate based on: -

1. The release of sensitive and harmful information about the target, even though such information is true;
2. The dissemination of information about the target which is based on a truth, but this is then exaggerated and magnified in order to create a distorted picture;
3. The fabrication of facts about the target.

Whether you became a target and victim of a narcissist's smear campaign is very much dependent on your position in relation to this narcissist. We regard those we interact with as sources of fuel. Fuel is what drives our kind and is the emotional reaction directed towards us by a person or persons. People are divided into three categories of source: -

1. The primary source. The most important person from the narcissist's point of view. Almost always the person chosen as an intimate partner;

2. The secondary source. Family, colleagues, inner and outer circle friends.
3. The tertiary source. Acquaintances, minions, remote stranger and strangers.

Those people in the secondary and tertiary sources (collectively the supplementary sources) are not often the target of a smear campaign. This is for several reasons: -

1. The relevant individual is performing his or her role without disobedience or difficulty and this meets with the narcissist's approval. This role is to provide fuel, carry out the wishes and desires of the narcissist and to provide character traits which our kind is able to purloin for our own use.
2. The level of interaction with the secondary and tertiary sources is not as great as with the primary, so therefore those secondary and tertiary sources are less likely to cross the narcissist;
3. The secondary and tertiary sources play a pivotal role in the maintenance of our façade, namely the presentation to the world at large that we are decent, honest, kind and generous people. A view which is at odds with the person who the primary source is exposed to during the devaluation period.
4. A secondary or tertiary source may well be jettisoned and replaced without the need for a smear campaign. We may regard it as a

better application of our energies by dropping and replacing than by smearing.

Accordingly, our friends, our neighbours, the person who serves us regularly in a bar, colleagues and so forth may not find themselves ever subjected to the smear campaign. I detail below when it may be deployed against these categories of people.

A smear campaign is mostly, although not exclusively used against the person who has been selected as the primary source. This person was selected to provide fuel to us regularly, without interruption and of a high quality. That is why this person was subjected to an intense and dizzying seduction. The smear campaign is an instrument of control. It is an instrument of fuel extraction. It is a cruel and vicious method of denigrating an individual further and is used in a variety of circumstances and with significant and devastating effect.

I am a narcissist and therefore I have used smear campaigns of all types against many different people with various outcomes, all those outcomes however being something that I have desired. As a narcissist I know how these campaigns are used, why they are used, why they are so effective and also what can be done to diminish their effect and indeed derail them. I have the inside knowledge on this staple weapon in the narcissist's arsenal and I willing to share this information with you. What you decide to do with it is entirely a matter for you but I can state with considerable authority that you will not find such a level of insight and enlightenment elsewhere so readily. I am compelled to write about all aspects of my behaviours, thoughts and machinations as a consequence of compulsory treatment which I must undertake. Accordingly, you find yourself in a special and privileged position having access to such knowledge.

In the body of this book I shall be addressing several key questions associated with the narcissistic smear campaign. These questions are as follows: -

What is a smear campaign?

When are smear campaigns used?

Why are they used?

Why are they so effective?

What effects do they have on you and on others?

Who is involved in the smear campaign?

What types of smear campaign exist?

How do you counter them?

This will be delivered in my customary no-nonsense style which enables you to get to the heart of the matter in an accessible and easily understandable way. Much of what I write will be uncomfortable to read but its capacity to assist you in knowing all about the narcissistic smear campaign and how to counter it is of huge value to you. I do not provide this information from a scientific perspective because that is not my expertise. There are many others who do so and there is naturally considerable value in the observations and opinions of the scientific community, I however prefer to provide you with my observations as a practitioner of the very thing which I am writing about in my direct manner. You may be used to reading similar compendiums about my kind couched either in scientific terms or the language of healing and therapy. You won't find that here. I am neither a scientific person, although I am of considerable intellect and I most certainly am not a healer, yet I know from the many comments of the readers of my other works that they have found considerable assistance in what I deliver in terms of their personalised approach to healing from the trauma of an encounter with our kind. As I often write, I tell you how it is, from my perspective and you as a free-thinking adult are entirely open to use it as you see fit.

What is a smear campaign?

A smear campaign is at its simplest a form of propaganda. The smear campaign is a concerted effort by a person or persons to discredit another person, group, organisation, business, race or country. Smear campaigns have been evident throughout history. They are designed to alter the way that another person or group thinks in order to cause them to oppose or turn away from that other person or group and in so doing assist the orchestrator of the smear campaign. There are thousands of examples of smear campaigns in the past. Some have been continuing for centuries, others are short-lived. Some occur just the once and with others they are repeated every so often. Smear campaigns have included:
-

- The Nazi campaign against the Jewish people and their religion;
- Richard II of England smearing the Irish as barbarians in order to gain support for an invasion of Ireland in the 14th century (interestingly it is believed that Richard suffered from a personality disorder himself)
- In the 1960s General Motors sought to smear the reputation of Ralph Nader, a prominent car safety campaigner;
- The Kremlin regularly accuses foreign powers of smearing the reputation of President Putin;
- In 1796 in the US Presidential election, John Adams was smeared by the Boston Independent Chronicle in what was most likely the

first smear campaign used in a US Presidential campaign although such tactics are used now at every election;

- In 2011 China sought to smear Apple through the use of advertisements in the press and on television

Smear campaigns are nowadays expected in political contests where one side will dig up some kind of dirt from the past of an opponent and use to show that this person is a liar, untrustworthy, is a hypocrite, once smoked drugs, once tried to ban guns and so on, in order to convince the electorate that this particular person is unfit for office and should not be elected. Smear campaigns are devised and operated by businesses to put rivals out of business. Smear campaigns are used by people to alienate others and win friendships.

A smear campaign uses untruths or the unfair use of the truth (out of context or exaggerated) to discredit a person in the eyes of others. In the context of its use by our kind it is invariably a campaign which is oral in nature. We like to use words because they are easy to use and can have a devastating effect. It does not take much effort for us to spew out some untruths about the victim of our campaign. Words also evaporate into the ether and allow us to deny ever saying them should you try to confront us about what we have been saying about you. Words are prone to being mis-heard, mis-interpreted and misunderstood all of which are advantages which we exploit in order to avoid accountability for our smears whilst propagating them against the victim. A smear campaign will arrive suddenly when used by us and its duration tends to be short. This is because we want it to appear without warning, be quickly circulated amongst those we are seeking to influence and have an immediate effect. Once that has been achieved we no longer need to keep fuelling the smear campaign. We will not retract it or correct the position but we have set it in motion and need not apply any further energy to it. This suits us as we like to conserve our energies. Indeed, many smear campaigns that we instigate take on a life of their own because people are natural gossips. They like to speculate about somebody, they like to engage in schadenfreude and they enjoy being the bearer of secret about somebody which they can then pass on to other people. Our smear campaigns usually acquire "legs" pretty quickly which enables us to sit back and watch the carnage unfold.

A smear campaign is all about backstabbing, lies, malicious falsehoods, pernicious comment and savage words about the person that we have in our sights. It is waged with sudden speed and intensity so that the victim is unaware that it is in progress and if they happen to become aware of the fact that it is in progress then they are unable to do much about it given the breakneck speed at which it is instigated. A smear campaign is one of the fundamental tools in our repertoire. It is easy to use, it is fast, it has the benefit of inherent deniability and its effects are manifold in terms of the benefit to us, the harm to the victim and the influence it has on others.

There must always be at least three parties to a smear campaign.

1. Us, the instigator;

2. A target, the person who is to be smeared; and

3. The audience, the people who are to be influenced by the smear campaign.

You may not realise this and I expand on it below, but you will form part of the audience during some of our smear campaigns. You may not realise that your participation in such an audience will ultimately come back to haunt you, but they will because those smear campaigns are necessary actions and devices as we move the relationship along in a way that suits us and will make our eventual smearing of you so much easier.

There are many different types of smear campaign and later I will be detailing some of these types so you are aware that these may be used against you at some point. It is worth pointing out that in the introduction I made reference to there being three ways in which a smear campaign is instigated. Either a sensitive or embarrassing secret is leaked and made widely known. This has the benefit of being true so that if a victim tried to threaten legal action for slander or libel, the defence of truth would avail itself to us and this is an absolute defence. Of course, you would regard the dissemination of this fact to be morally reprehensible but as I am sure you know by now out moral compass is not only way off the mark but we threw it away a long time ago. Another way the smear campaign is formed is to invent something about the target. This poses little difficulty for us with our astonishing capability for telling lies but does have the potential (although this does not largely concern us at the time given our attitude of never being to blame and never being accountable) for repercussions. The third way is to take a grain of truth and then use is out of context and/or exaggerate it in some way so that something trivial, albeit true, is regarded as problematic once magnified.

In order to use the first (leaking a truth) and the third (embellishing a truth) we must of course have access to that piece of truth in the first place. We acquire lots of information about you when we target you but the information which provides us with an arsenal to use against you at a later stage comes from you during the seduction period. Under the auspices of being caring and interested in you, we will milk you for as much information as we possibly can. We want to know all about the things you enjoy, the things you dislike, what makes you laugh, what makes you cry, who your friends are and who your enemies are. We want to know what keeps you awake at night, whether anything terrible has happened in your past, if there is some dark family secret applicable to you, whether there was an embarrassing incident at school, if there has been a shameful episode with a past lover and so forth. We question, probe and investigate in order to compile a dossier of such information. Any vulnerabilities and weaknesses on your part are never garnered because we care and we are compassionate. They are acquired because we want to make you think that we care and are compassionate (and in turn you become drawn to us) and most of all so that we can take these pieces of information about you and furnish them into weapons to use against you during devaluation. This gathered information is also used in the smear campaign that will be used against you in due course. Accordingly, you should be aware that when you are being question, no matter how caring or pleasant it may seem, anything that you provide which evidences some kind of vulnerability or weakness will be utilised against you in a smear campaign. You, in effect, become the architect of your own misfortune by offering up this information so easily. Of course you were not to know at that early juncture that our kind-hearted and passionate love was just an illusion to be used to draw you in. You know it now however and you are also in a position to warn those people that you care about who are just as susceptible as you to being entangled by our kind to be wary of such questioning for behind it lies a dark purpose.

The seeds of the smear campaign are actually sowed by you way back during the seduction and we gratefully accept those seeds which we carefully incubate ready to use as terrible, thorny plants to rip and tear your reputation to shreds at a later date.

When is the Smear Campaign Used?

This all depends on who the target of the smear campaign is. There are five main targets of our smear campaigns. These are as follows: -

1. The Defective Supplementary Source
2. The Troublemaker
3. The Predecessor Primary Source
4. The Primary Source
5. The Stigmatised Individual

You will no doubt be aware that we create a web and a network of fuel lines from various appliances to ourselves. These appliances are drawn from the primary and supplementary sources and cover people of differing relationships to us, ages, outlook, social background and such like. You may be in place as our primary source but we will also be extracting fuel from your predecessor, your friends, our friends, colleagues, family members, strangers on the internet, stranger in a bar, people we nod to at work and so on. Lots of different fuel lines which we draw on at different times and to different degrees. They will be in place when you are targeted by us and when your relationship commences and develops with us when you have been installed as our primary source.

The first three occasions when the smear campaign is used can happen at any time during your relationship (as primary source) with us. From the very outset all the way through you may witness (although prior to reading this book you will not have realised that this is what they are) smear campaigns being instigated and maintained against various targets. You should pay heed to this. In common with our ability to make something appear different to what it actually is, we will mask these smear campaigns and make them seem like the appropriate responses by us to the behaviour of the target and every time you will accept this as being correct. You will accept our explanations because you will be in the grip of the golden period where everything about us is wonderful, magnificent and sensational so that you lose your ability to critically evaluate what is actually happening because you believe everything that we say. Indeed, this brain-washing is instrumental in ensuring that these smear campaigns are actually effective. Not only will you not question us for doing them but you will support the action that is being taken because we will dress it up as being a necessary action for the continued maintenance of our happy and ecstatic union. Turning to each of the above categories.

1. The Defective Supplementary Source

This may be a friend, a colleague or a family member. It may include someone who serves us regularly in a shop or someone we know through a chat room. These people are drawn to us through our outward façade of charm, magnificence and apparent goodness. We then draw fuel from them, have them carry out our bidding and/or provide us with traits that we claim as our own. These people are necessary in respect of the way that we function. If they become defective this is because: -

a. They have diminished the amount of fuel they provide us;
b. They have stopped providing us with fuel;
c. They will not do what we want;
d. They have nothing to offer us anymore;
e. They have challenged us;
f. They have seen through us.

I call a-f above as the Offending Acts.

The commission of an Offending Act will mean the appliance is designated as defective and then there will be either discard and replacement or the instigation of a smear campaign against the offending defective appliance.

This person may have stopped praising us as often as they once did because they regard the nature of the relationship as one which is long-lasting and on familiar terms. They still like us but they do not respond as often to our texts fishing for compliments or they are often busy when we invite them to join us for drinks. This diminution in fuel suggests that we are no longer as important to us. It might be that they have formed new social circles and therefore have less time available for us, they may have work or family commitments. Certainly from their point of view they will not regard themselves as having done anything wrong. They will admit they may not see me as much as they once did but they will not regard this as weakening the relationship. We do. We need to be able to rely on such people to provide fuel when we require it and if the occasions when they do so have reduced or we see them just as regularly but our initial charm has become less mesmerising so their provision of fuel is reduced then we regard them as defective.

The relevant person may have actually stopped providing us with fuel. This will be because they have moved away or it might be that work and/or domestic commitments have taken a priority over socialising. They may have experienced some kind of life change (a new relationship/marriage/ children) which alters their focus and their attention is placed elsewhere. Their fuel stops and shows no sign of being resurrected. Accordingly, this person is deemed as defective.

It may be the case that the relevant person has stopped doing what we want. Their compliance may manifest in different ways such as lending us money, providing clients for our work, getting us invited to certain events, letting us stay at their house, carrying out tasks on our behalf, assisting us with our manipulation of others. We regard those in the position of supplementary sources as servants who are to do what we want. If they no longer do this – be it through moving away from us, no longer having that compliance in their gift (e.g. they do not earn as much as they once did or they cannot accommodate us any longer) or simply because they have decided that they do not want to do that thing for us any longer because it has them drained, unappreciated and/or feeling used, then they are labelled as defective.

The person may not be able to offer us anything more as a consequence of something happening that is outside of their control. They may move jobs and therefore move to a different place so they cannot allow us to use their house for our trysts with a new prospective primary source. They may have lost their job so they cannot lend money to us. They may have changed positions in a company so they are not in a position to do us favours. The person may have fallen ill and therefore is unable to function as they once did. There are many different reasons why they can no longer benefit us. They did not choose this but it has happened and accordingly their use to us has been altered meaning that they are a defective appliance.

It may be the case that the person has challenged us in some way. They may not have liked the way we have treated them, leant on them, pressured them and such like. They may be dismayed at the manner in which we have treated another member of the family or a friend. Accordingly, they have challenged our behaviour and sought to usurp our status and authority. This cannot be countenanced. We may be able to bring about compliance by the swift application of a manipulation or through the application of our ignited fury, but if we cannot then this person is deemed a defective appliance.

The final instance where a member of the supplementary sources becomes a defective appliance is where the person has seen through us. They may not actually realise that we are a narcissist but they have recognised that we care only for ourselves, use them and others and generally engage in self-serving behaviour. This is more than just challenging us. Challenging us when an appliance refuses to do one specific thing or accuses us of behaving in one certain way. Seeing through us is when the appliance attacks our very character. Not only have they ceased to provide fuel but there is a risk that they are criticising us with the horrendous consequences which arise from that.

Thus, these are the circumstances which result in a person from the supplementary sources being deemed to be a defective appliance. The starting point is to usually discard them. They have served their purpose; they are defective so they are jettisoned. It is more important to obtain a replacement, maintain the façade and the provision of positive fuel from the replacement than devalue you the defective appliance. Indeed, if the cessation of fuel and/or failure to be of benefit to us has arisen because they have moved away then instigating a devaluation against them may actually prove costlier in terms of energy expenditure than the fuel that would be yielded. We simply decide to let these people go.

There are however other instances where a smear campaign is required against this defective appliance. This arises in the following circumstances: -

1. We still have to interact with this person. This is usually the case when the defective appliance is a family member of colleague. They have become defective but we still see them occasionally at events, family gatherings, work and so on. They serve no purpose to us but their repeated appearance is a reminder of their defective

status which offends us. Accordingly, we instigate a smear campaign to discredit them (and thus explain why we no longer talk etc.), to garner sympathy for our position (and thus fuel), to maintain the façade and also with the potential to gather negative fuel from the target of the campaign. I expand in greater detail below as to why we apply the smear campaign against this person but those are the main reasons why. If we have to deal with them, we may as well make it worth our while and provoke some negative fuel from them;

2. We want to punish the person for their lack of loyalty;

3. They become a troublemaker and threaten to pollute the minds of other sources that supply us and/or form part of our façade. This person is dangerous and they must be isolated and discredited through the application of the smear campaign.

The timing of this smear campaign can be at any point with regard to these supplementary sources. They will ordinarily bask in the golden period but if they commit one of the acts above which causes them to be labelled as defective then this means that if they are not discarded then the smear campaign will occur. It may be after a month of knowing them it could be years and it can happen at any time in terms of your relationship with us as the primary source. The fact we have been friends with someone for ten years or the person is our brother does not matter. If they commit and Offending Act, they are labelled as defective and it is either discard or smear.

2. The Troublemaker

You may think that someone who has been labelled a defective appliance because they have challenged us or seen through us would be regarded as a troublemaker. They are but not in the context of this categorisation. Defective appliances are those people who we managed to charm and seduce who then failed us in some way. The Troublemaker is somebody who we have failed to seduce, failed to get "onside" and therefore they have the capacity to derail our plans, cause us problems, question our status and behaviours and attempt to influence other people (and especially the new primary source) against us or at least not do what we want.

The Troublemaker can appear in various forms: -

a. A member of your group of friends;

b. A member of your family

c. A member of our family who we reluctantly have to deal with;

d. The odd one out in a group we have attached to us. For instance, we may join a local charity committee and everybody on that committee bar one regards us as a good person. This one person has reservations (unfounded naturally!) about our bona fides and therefore this person whilst part of the group owing to him or being on the committee, it regarded as a Trouble Maker;

e. There are new recruits to the team or department at work and one or more do not fall under our seductive spell;

f. Somebody on a sporting team does not "buy into" our way of operating and thinking.

These Trouble Makers are either linked to you ("Affiliated") or somebody we have had "forced" upon us ("Add-On").

Our need to control all of those around us to a greater or letter degree is necessary. It also means that like a dictatorship we cannot allow for dissenting voices. These dissenters not only amount to trouble in themselves but they also have the concerning capacity to make other people review their stance towards us, revise their opinions and alter their behaviours.

If we have selected you as a primary source, we also want your friends, family, colleagues thinking we are wonderful, pleasant and decent as well. Many will be won over easily, some with a little more effort but if there is a dissenter then this cannot be tolerated. This person is not often somebody we can discard because they have not become part of our coterie. In the category above, those people who provided fuel and served a purpose formed part of our obedient coterie. If they stopped, they are ejected from the coterie and are replaced unless there is a reason to reject them and embark on a smear campaign. In this category, the relevant person was never under out control or influence to begin with. This then means that we are not in a positon to discard them. Furthermore, they may, much to out annoyance, have an established "right" to remain inside our sphere but remain uninfluenced. It may be your best friend, your sister, a work colleague, somebody on our team, somebody we have to work with and so forth. We have to, initially at least, tolerate that person's presence.

The smear campaign will be unleashed against this individual as soon as we identify that they will not be charmed by us and that they have the potential to cause us difficulties. It is one or the other. In common with our black and white thinking, you are either on Team Narcissist or you are not. If you are not, you are a Trouble Maker and you will have a smear campaign unleashed against you.

If you are our primary source, you will witness and also be involved in, the application of a smear campaign against this Trouble Maker. The aim (which will be expanded on below) is to isolate, drive out and/or nullify their trouble-making influence on our machinations and manipulations. They must be ring-fenced, neutralised and pushed to one side or even better, completely away.

If the Trouble Maker is linked to you as my primary source (e.g. your friend, colleague or family member) I will involve you in the smear campaign to increase its effect and ensure success. If the Trouble Maker arrives as an add-on (e.g. team member, committee member and such like) you are unlikely to be directly involved but you will see it happen during our relationship.

The appearance of a Trouble Maker affiliated with you will mean that you see this particular smear campaign at the outset of our relationship. Add-On Trouble Makers will be smeared at any time during our relationship, as and when they present themselves.

3. The Predecessor Primary Source

This is usually our immediate ex-partner but it may also include ex partners even further back. We always smear your predecessor who was the primary source before you. You are the main audience for this smear campaign. The predecessor will be labelled as abusive, a stalker, crazy, intolerant, mental, dangerous, obsessed and many more things besides. The smear campaign against your predecessor will commence early on in your relationship with our kind. It is more likely than not that as we commence our seduction of you we are still engaged in a relationship with them as we insure against the loss of fuel by developing you as a source of positive fuel ready to be coupled to us once we determine you make the grade to be a primary source whilst we still keep extracting negative fuel from the outgoing and soon to be discarded incumbent. At this cross-over point there may be no mention of anybody else to you. Alternatively, we may refer to the incumbent as the ex even though they have not yet been discarded in order to maximise our prospects with you. If the ex is mentioned, then the smear campaign against them will begin starting with you as the audience. If we decide against mentioning the ex to you until the discard has happened, then the smear campaign against that person will begin then. Either way you can expect to observe a smear campaign against the soon-to-be ex or ex. You will of course not recognise it as a smear campaign but rather a heartfelt explanation from a hurt and wounded person who has tried to do their best with a difficult and disordered individual only to be lashed out at, wounded and abused. It will appear both as a method of seducing you and also a method of smearing them and this is expanded on further in the following chapter.

Accordingly, you will witness (but not recognise) smear campaigns against your predecessor and also a Trouble Maker (especially if they are an Affiliated Trouble Maker) close to the outset of your relationship with our kind where you are the new primary source. During our relationship you will then also witness smear campaigns against Defective Supplementary Sources, some of whom you may have come to know rather well.

The fourth category in terms of determining when a smear campaign will take place concerns the primary source which more often than not, will be applicable to you as a reader of this book.

4. The Primary Source

The smear campaign against a primary source takes place close to the point of discard. We have decided that we no longer want to be involved with you in terms of a relationship. Whether this is as romantic partners, friends, colleagues or a family member, we do not want to have to engage with you on the expected terms. You may remain a member of the family and related to us but we do not want to deal with you any longer. Of course our connection will never be completely severed because we always reserve the right to come back and hoover you. However, at this juncture we have decided that the current arrangement is at an end. We have various reasons for effecting a discard – you may have challenged us, you may be beginning to see through us but usually it is because you are not providing us with the fuel that we want to the degree we want and therefore you have also become a defective appliance. This is of greater concern because as our primary source you are meant to be the provider of fuel at a greater level and potency that all other sources and therefore when you fail to do so this creates a considerable concern in us. Once this happens and we have put in place (of hopefully have put in place) an alternative primary source then you will be discarded. Shortly before this happens, a matter of days usually, we will commence our smear campaign against you. I detail below why this is done and how this is done but so far as you are concerned you will not know about it (unless you happen to be tipped off) until after you have been discarded. You must then deal with the disorientation caused by this callous discard along with the vicious nature of the smear campaign.

If you have escaped us and managed to do this without providing us with a chance to unleash a Preventative Hoover to stop you going and/or you resist our Initial Grand Hoover, then the smear campaign will follow straight afterwards along with Malign Follow-Up Hoovers (see **Black Hole** for more information on the types of hoovers and the rationale behind them and their effects). If you have been especially effective and planned your departure, kept it hidden from us and then executed it on your terms then there is the possibility that the smear campaign may not actually happen. I detail more about this in the chapter concerning countering the smear campaign. If it still does happen, it will follow very soon after a failed Initial Grand Hoover. If we believe we can hoover you back in after you have escape, we will not instigate a smear campaign until such time as we have tried the Initial Grand Hoover.

5. The Stigmatised Individual

This is a somewhat different smear campaign that we effect. Truth be told that when we smear anybody they become stigmatised but this fifth category is in respect of a particular set of circumstances. The Stigmatised Individual is a smear campaign which is most often found in a familial environment and is used by a narcissistic individual against members of the family. It could be against a parent, a sibling but most often it used against a child. The stigmatisation will begin in childhood and will continue through into adulthood as the victim is regarded as "a bad penny", "the black sheep of the family" and similar labels.

Whilst the individual will suffer character assassinations from our kind (the character assassination being the direct and face-to-face version of the smear campaign) for the most part the victim may be utterly unaware of the fact that they have suffered this smear campaign and have done so for years, even decades. When used in the case of a child, the narcissistic parent will smear the child to other siblings, to the other parent, to other relations, friends, teachers and so forth. Comments such as these are familiar.

"He has been a considerable disappointment to me."

"She never listens to me."

"I have tried to deal with his bad behaviour but it is such hard work."

"I don't know where she gets such insolence from and with such a good upbringing."

"He is a trouble maker. That's all there is to it."

"He will never amount to much."

"If there is a problem, she is behind it."

"She is such a drama queen."

"He is just downright disobedient."

The frequent reinforcement of comments such as these and others create the image in the mind of the recipient that the child is badly-behaved, wild, insolent, self-centred, unlikely to achieve, disrespectful and so on. The child will often be unaware of this tarring that is going on but all around are infected with the untruths pedalled by the narcissistic parent. This parent will pick and choose evidence in support of this hypothesis that they have created. The parent is projecting their own failures and insecurities onto the child in order to ensure that he or she is not accountable for them. Furthermore, this stigmatisation is designed to draw fuel from the audience in quantities greater than that which the child might provide if it were made aware of the ongoing smear campaign against it. In a way, the parent (or sibling etc.) is creating a reverse façade whereby from an early age the victim is being labelled so that as the child grows, the relevant narcissist can then use the reverse façade as a means of drawing fuel over and over again.

At some point the child, usually when an adult, will learn the full extent of the stigmatisation that has taken place but by then it is so entrenched and ingrained that tackling it is nigh on impossible

This stigmatisation is a form of smear campaign but it differs from those usually perpetrated by the narcissist for the following reasons: -

- It originates usually in childhood. The other smear campaigns are utilised in adulthood;
- It is extensive in time period;
- It is the smear campaign which is least likely to tip-off the victim for a considerable period of time. Both the narcissist and the audience say nothing to the victim because he or she is still a child;
- The narcissist is more interested in the dynamic with the audience that the victim. The fuel is drawn from the audience with the fuel coming from the victim at a later stage.
- The impact of this type of smear campaign is especially entrenched and reinforced and very difficult for the victim to tackle.
- Whilst there is often an element of projection and blame-shifting with smear campaigns, it is especially prevalent in this stigmatisation.

It should also be borne in mind that the narcissist you are involved with may well have been subjected to such stigmatisation and this will be a material factor not only in their overall behaviour towards you, but their own use of the smear campaign. This discussion, of how being a recipient of a smear campaign him or herself in childhood affects the narcissist, is for another time.

Accordingly, dependent on who the smear campaign is directed at, they will happen at different times. Viewed from the perspective of the primary source you will see them at the outset of your relationship with us, during your relationship and in respect of you, at the end. In terms of the stigmatisation of an individual you may not witness this unless you are the victim or you come into contact with the affected individual (the sibling, parent, child or other relative of the narcissist you are entangled with.) Of course, ordinarily you will have little idea that these are actually smear campaigns.

Why are Smear Campaigns Used?

It is necessary for you to understand why the smear campaign is used. Whenever you understand the reasons why something is said or done it enables you to deal with it in a much more effective way. It is akin to being involved in a physical fight with somebody. If you cannot see them, it is that much harder to fight them. By preventing you from understanding why we do things, we make it feel like you are fighting an invisible opponent. You do not know where the next blow might be coming from. This confusion, bewilderment and lack of comprehension exists throughout much of your entanglement with us. Indeed, ensuring you do not understand what is happening to you forms a huge part of why our manipulations are so effective. By gaining understanding, you remove anxiety and apprehension and you gain the tools required for addressing it and countering it. If you do not know why something is happening, how can you be expected to deal with it? This is equally applicable to dealing with the smear campaigns that we deploy. Once you understand the rationale for them it will remove the unknown and thus diminish your anxiety but it will also enable you to consider (along with what is contained in the final chapter) how to counter the smears.

This understanding requires consideration of who the target of the smear is because we have different reasons for our behaviour dependent on who we are flinging that mud at.

1. The Defective Supplementary Source

The defective supplementary source will be smeared in order to prevent this person from affecting your view (if you are our primary source) of us. It will often be the case that the defective supplementary source will feel the need to attack us and who better to do that to than the primary source? Of course, the defective individual does not know that you are our primary source but rather than you are our intimate partner and the defective person will feel a considerable need, once discarded by us, to attack us to our face but also to tell you how awful we are as well in the hope of damaging our relationship. In order to prevent a hammer blow being struck against our primary source, someone which we must defend for the purposes of extracting fuel, we will smear the defective person so that their word is not believed. They will be portrayed as jealous and a fantasist who has bitten the hand that has fed it and when reprimanded does not like it. The smear will be done just prior to this person being discarded or around the same time so that when they try and fight back and persuade you that: -

"He is just after one thing from you."

"He is a nasty bastard. You will see."

"You want to get away from the likes of him."

"It will all end in tears, it always does with someone like him."

"He will soon tire of you; you know? He always does."

"He will make you suffer. Mark my words."

You will dismiss the comments of a ranting and unbalanced individual.

The defective person is also smeared for the purposes of extracting fuel from them. Once they become aware of what is being said about them by me (and others who are involved in instigating the smear campaign (see below) their reaction will invariably be one of amazement, anger, upset, irritation, denial and so forth. We may not see the reaction but we know what it will be, based on our knowledge of the individual concerned and the way our smear campaigns usually work. Accordingly, we still obtain fuel from knowing how this person will be reacting to the smear campaign. It is even better if they challenge us by confronting us in person or on the telephone as their bitter protestations or angry retorts just fuel us further.

The defective person must also be smeared to prevent other people (not just you as our primary source) from thinking ill of us. We do not want a rotten apple in our coterie affecting all of our other loyal supporters. The dissenter must be silenced and the instigation of a smear campaign is one of the most effective ways of achieving this. By stripping that person of any credibility we are in a far better position to ensure that it is our message that is listened to. We have the advantage also of being able to call on our supporters (see a later chapter for who those people are) and thus through force of numbers we are able to smear the dissenting individual and rely on the time-proven (although of course not necessarily accurate) approach that those in the minority must of course be wrong because why else would they be in the minority?

A defective person is also subjected to a smear campaign as a consequence of the need to punish them for failing to accord with their chosen role. This is less likely to be a response from the Lesser and Mid-Range of our kind and more likely to occur if the defective person has crossed one of the Greater of our brethren. The punishment is justified in our minds because this person has failed in their allocated role and therefore it is only right that he or she is punished for this failure. Furthermore, it sends out a clear signal to the balance of our supporters that should you ever cross us, fail us or speak out against us as this dissenter has done, then you can expect the same treatment. Thus we maintain the image we wish to present and anybody who might think about speaking out against us will readily think twice before doing so.

2. The Trouble Maker

The smear campaign is used against the trouble maker in order to isolate the individual. You will recall that this person has not fallen from grace like the defective appliance, this person never attained a position of grace to begin with. Utilising our emotional intelligence, we are able to ascertain those people who have reservations about us. If this is an individual who we are trying to gain fuel from in a day-to-day situation we will soon realise that there is none to be gained (or it will cost too much energy to obtain it) and therefore we will disengage from this person and pick somebody else. We do not have to engage with the person who was not susceptible to our overtures. The trouble maker is someone we have to deal with because they are either affiliated through you as a primary source or they are an add-on and we have no option other than to tolerate their presence. We cannot from the beginning tell your friend they are not welcome – this would alert you and result in additional problems. We cannot just decree that a person should be removed from the committee as this would be unlikely to work and in all likelihood could cause opinion to turn against us. We are saddled with this particular person. They have reservations about us, they have not warmed to us or they may even have an inkling about what we are. There are various degrees of this but ultimately they will not embrace out seduction and fall in with the spell we have cast over you and others. Thus they are marked out as a trouble maker. They must be isolated so that their opinions are not only able to be voiced far less frequently (because you as our primary source do not engage with them as often) and when they do you are less likely to listen to them. The smear campaign achieves this isolation.

The smear campaign is also used against the trouble-maker to prevent damage to the façade. We have constructed that careful world image of ourselves and we do not want somebody whose presence we have to tolerate chipping away at that image and fracturing the façade. The longer that person is allowed to remain in a position of some influence and the longer they are allowed to air their concerns, reservations and observations, call them what you will, the greater the risk that people will actually listen to them and give them credence. This will damage the façade and not only strip us of supporters but damage and possibly remove a significant instrument of fuel extraction, control and manipulation. The façade must be preserved and having a trouble maker affecting it cannot be countenanced.

The smear campaign is also unleashed against the trouble maker to prevent them from de-railing the seduction. Our seduction of you is intense and powerful but in its early stages, as we are sinking our hooks into you, there is a risk that you may be persuaded to examine our motives in a clearer fashion. You may be shown the multitude of red flags which are flying and therefore be able to evade us. We do not like to lose. We do not like our carefully prepared and orchestrated seductions to fail. If there is somebody whispering in your ear about us, pointing out the red flags, sounding the klaxons and raising the alarm they must be dealt with. The smear campaign tackles such a trouble maker and reduces and removes the risk that may present to our successful seduction of you.

The smear campaign is also used to draw fuel from this trouble maker. Unusually it will be negative fuel at such an early stage. With you as our primary source, our supporters and those which we are recruiting from your supporters, we draw positive fuel. This trouble maker has offered no positive fuel but we are not going to let them off the hook. We want to isolate them, render them ineffective and for putting us to the trouble of instigating a smear campaign against them we want some reward and that will be fuel. We will typically triangulate them as well during the smear campaign so we show that you and others are listening to us and not them, whilst piling on the untruths about them. Their reaction, usually anger and upset, will provide us with negative fuel which we gladly accept by way as compensation for their awkwardness in trying to turn people against us.

3. The Predecessor

The predecessor is smeared for a number of reasons. Firstly, it is also the case that we must preserve the façade. We do not want an old flame contacting those within our supporters and telling the uncomfortable truth about us so accordingly we need to ensure that they are not believed when they do and thus they are subjected to a smear campaign.

Furthermore, if anybody is going to harm our seduction of you it is an embittered predecessor. They will be bristling from their recent discard. They will want the truth to be told about us and this desire will power them in terms of wanting to get even with us. We do not want them dedicating their energies to a campaign that unmasks us as we are seducing you. We may have made a good start in terms of sliding our tendrils around you but there will still be work to do and therefore we do not want this seduction to unravel because of what the predecessor has to say. Of course the predecessor, better than anybody (including you at this stage) knows just what we are really like and how we truly behave. They will still bear the emotional and physical scars from our abrasive devaluation of them and the heartless discard that followed. They will be able to recount, to anybody willing to listen, with considerable detail and recall, all of the golden period and then the vicious devaluation that followed. They can refer to events, instances, times and so forth which adds credibility to their tales. Accordingly, this body of evidence could deal a fatal blow to our seduction of you by causing you to get cold feet. Moreover, if we are of a lesser kind, this kind of threat when combined with you questioning us about what has happened in a fashion which shows you are giving the allegations some credence may cause a loss of control by the lesser. This means the mask will slip very early on and the appearance of the beast lurking beneath combined with the predecessor's allegations are likely to cause you to realise that we are not what you thought we were before the effects of our seduction and the golden period have worked their addictive magic on you. Thus there is a risk for the lesser that you will accept the predecessor's allegations and retreat from the seduction. This will leave the lesser in a chaotic position with not only the wounds from the predecessor's criticism and from your criticism of us by rejecting the seduction, it also means there is no primary source of fuel and thus a lesser in such a situation will be placed in a particularly perilous position. Accordingly, it is fundamental for any such risk from the predecessor to the success of the seduction to be reduced and hopefully extinguished. Hence the smear campaign.

The smear campaign against the predecessor is also used for a positive reason in respect of you as the new prospect. By making out that the predecessor is some jealous, crazed creature you will be bound to us more tightly for fear of the malicious attacks which may arise from this predecessor. You are likely to feel sorry for us after hearing the nature of the smear campaign- for example we will often claim the predecessor was abusive – and therefore the sympathy that gushes from you is not only wonderful fuel for us, it also means that you want to be with us, make us happy, protect us and keep us away from such a horrible person. Thus the smear campaign is used not only to prevent damage to the seduction but it is also used for the purposes of maximising the success of the seduction too.

Finally, the smearing of the predecessor is done to draw fuel. In this instance it is most likely to allow us to draw two lots of fuel. Firstly, from you as a consequence of your affection, sympathy and concern that we have had to put up with such an awful person beforehand. Secondly from the predecessor themselves since they will always react in an emotional fashion to the smear campaign. That person is still raw from their entanglement with us. The devaluation looms large in their mind, along with the discard and possible hoovers that followed. Their emotional toughness has been eroded and it does not take much from us to know exactly how to cause them to erupt in an emotional fashion so we can draw fuel from their tears, anger, fear and frustration. It should also be borne in mind that the predecessor may well have found themselves subjected to two smear campaigns.

In some instances, we have begun to seduce you as the replacement as we prepare to discard the incumbent who will be the predecessor.

There is a cross-over between the two of you. You are already involved with us, but not yet the primary source. Once you have been anointed in this position and the incumbent is discarded then they are also smeared. This serves the purposes outlined above.

In other cases, the predecessor may have escaped us and our attempt to hoover them failed. They are smeared as part of the smearing of the primary source. We then rely on supplementary sources for fuel as we try to find and install a new primary source. As we identify you and court you we are aware that the predecessor, whilst having no desire to return to us, wishes us to do us harm through speaking to you as the new prospect and therefore it becomes necessary to smear them again, this time as part of a predecessor smear. This double dosage of smearing will result in the target proving particularly emotional in his or her responses.

4. The Primary Source of Fuel

It is the primary source who suffers the brunt of smear campaigns. Whereas a defective appliance may be jettisoned and replaced and thus spared such a campaign, the primary source almost always (unless they have been fortunate enough to take pre-emptive action – see below) will suffer a smear campaign. The trouble maker will experience one but not on the same scale as the primary source. The predecessor will suffer one also and whilst it is scathing in nature it is not like that meted out to the primary source of fuel.

Your importance as the primary source means that the disappointment that follows when you fail to function as required results in your smear being fiercer and more hurtful than the other types.

Firstly, there is a risk that following your discard you may damage the façade by trying to tell everyone what we are like. Given the extensive knowledge that you are privy to, you pose a greater risk than the defective appliance or the trouble maker and therefore our need to neutralise your risk is greater than usual in order to protect the precious façade.

Secondly, the smear seeks to squeeze those last drops of fuel from you as we denigrate you further. We are able to visualise your distress (which is heightened owing to the combination of the still-felt effects of the devaluation and the recent discard combining with the nasty nature of the smear) and therefore the level of fuel that stands to be obtained from you in this last act as you are discarded is significant.

Thirdly, there is an element of punishment which arises, especially from the Greater of our kind. You have failed us. You either failed to comply with the role that we have assigned you or even worse you have sought to escape us and cause massive disruption to our fuel supply. Either way you should be punished and the smear campaign is the result of this reason to punish you.

Fourthly, the smear campaign is used as an instrument of control. We may have discarded you for now but this does not mean that we are entirely done with you. Not only do we reserve the right to hoover you, we want to show you that we still, even when you have been jettisoned have control over you by making you angry, miserable, frightened and upset through the application of the smear campaign. The fact we can still do this and achieve such an outcome to someone we have pushed to one side underlines our power. Even if you have escaped us, your reaction to our smear campaign still allows us to exert power over you, despite your treachery.

Fifthly, the smear campaign is an extremely useful primer for a hoover. If we discarded you and smeared you, you may still want us back. If the smear campaign is vicious you want relief from it. You want relief from the pain of: -

a. The devaluation and its continuing effects;
b. The nature of the discard; and
c. The recent (maybe ongoing) smear campaign.

You just want it to stop. This means that if we offer you a hand back towards being with us, if we usher you towards the open door through which you can see the glow of the golden period, you are far more susceptible to being hoovered so that you can stop the pain.

Even if you escaped us, the application of a smear campaign and its cruel misery may well enable us to tenderise you in readiness for an Initial Grand Hoover or Benign Follow-up Hoovers in order to bring you back to us. The opportunity to end the pain may well prove too great to resist.

5. The Stigmatised Individual

The use of a smear campaign against this individual, as I have mentioned above, usually being a family member given the length of time the smearing takes place over and the fact that the victim has little or no chance of escaping it (since he or she is a child and also often he or has no idea it is being done) during its application. The key reasons why a smear campaign is used against this victim are as follows: -

- The projection of the narcissist's own failings and insecurities. Whilst there is often an element of projection in smear campaigns, it is heightened with regards to stigmatisation;
- The need to exert control over the victim by creating a reverse façade which the audience become aware of so that they alter their treatment of the victim;
- The provision of fuel. Principally this comes from the audience (since the victim is unaware of this slow-burning smear) but eventually once the victim gains awareness and rails against this, the victim will provide fuel as well;
- The creation of an entrenched and difficult to destroy smear. The fact it has been in place for years means that the victim has a near impossible task of undoing the effects of the smear on his or her reputation;
- Providing a contrast for the narcissist to elevate and laud a relative of the victim. This is often seen as the victim being the black sheep and another child being regarded as the favourite or golden

child. A brother may have a blackened sister and a golden sister. Similarly, the narcissist may behave in a similar way with one parent over another;

- This allows the narcissist greater control over the family dynamic by applying a divide and conquer approach using the smear campaign as the main method of achieving this.

Accordingly, the rationale for our smear campaigns depends on when those smear campaigns are taking place and in particular the person against whom they are aimed. By understanding the reasons why these smear campaigns happen, your anxiety and sense of being trapped by the unknown is reduced and you are placed in a better position to now know what to do about it.

Why Are Smear Campaigns So Effective?

It is highly likely that you have been on the receiving end of a smear campaign, if you are reading this book. It is unusual if such a campaign is not used by our kind when dealing with the person who holds the position of primary source of fuel. The benefits of instigating the smear campaign are numerous and indeed in many instances the smear campaign is a necessary device for the maintenance of appearances, fuel and control. I have detailed above several reasons why smear campaigns are used and they are used because not only are they effective, they are affective at achieving a number of outcomes for our kind. Since we are creatures of economy when it comes to the expenditure of our energies we operate those manipulations which are the most rewarding in terms of energy versus effectiveness. If the smear campaign did not have such a high degree of efficacy, we would not bother with it. The fact that people like us do so, demonstrates in itself how effective they are. It is necessary, as you have learned why the smear campaigns are used, for you to also grasp what it is about them that is so effective so you can then organise yourself appropriate to counter them. Some of the reason for this effectiveness is down to us and some of it is caused by you and certainly in that regard you need to be aware what it is that you do that contributes to their effectiveness. There are seven reasons underpinning the effectiveness of smear campaigns.

1. Conviction

The smear campaign is rolled out in a convincing fashion. It is done with speed, it is done for the most part without your knowledge and it is effected by us in a manner which suggests that our words are undeniable truth. We are very good at persuading and portraying something as correct and the truth when it is not. We will seize on some element of your behaviour, some aspect of actions on your part or things you have said which are recognised by people. Perhaps you once got drunk at a party and kept falling over (it was a one-off and not helped by the fact you hadn't eaten beforehand the copious amounts of alcohol we plied you with) but this forms the basis of creating a picture of your abusive alcoholic actions. You may be known for getting over emotional, especially when tired and therefore the picture is painted of you as histrionic. Taking some germ of truth and then applying it out of context, exaggerating and magnifying is a skill we utilise in the creation of the smear campaign.

"Yes, I am afraid I am at my wit's end with Jenny, her drinking is out of control. I have kept a lid on it so far for your sake, I didn't know want you upset, but I do not know what to do. You remember that party at Jonathan's? Yes, that's right when she could not even sit up, that's a nightly occurrence now."

We speak with such conviction and confidence that people do not challenge what we say. People usually accept the truth of what they are told by other people. This is a necessary social device because if it was to the contrary nothing would get done if people were suspicious and question everybody's motives and comments. We play on this default setting and our confident and superior nature allows us to create a convincing smear campaign and thus guarantee its effectiveness.

Bear in mind the fact that our smear campaigns will be supported by other people (see chapter below) and this body of numbers provides greater authority so that anybody who may be wavering would rather join the club as opposed to trying to beat it. People have a herd mentality and it takes a particularly rigorous sense of integrity and strength of character to stand up in protest to something, more so if you are alone or in the minority. It is far easier to accept what the majority are saying and secure yourself a peaceful life. Furthermore, if you are amongst our supporters and you know what happens to those who cross us, you do not want to suffer the same fate and it thus becomes far easier to agree. With so many people operating in this fashion, through threat or fear of isolation, it is easy enough for us to get sufficient numbers agreeing with us and carried on this tide of majority opinion the strength of our conviction increases.

2. The Façade

Our façade of respectability that we have carefully created whereby we are seen as good, reliable, dependable and kind to the outside world provides us with serious support when doing out a smear campaign. In the similar way by which we point to evidence of your drink problem, temper tantrums and neediness as the basis for a much larger and wide problem, we rely on the existence of the constructed façade to demonstrate that we are not the issue. How can we be? We are seen by your friends, the neighbours and your family as that generous, pleasant and helpful chap who must be a good husband and father. He always says hello, is polite, holds down a good job, is seen out and about in the community and so forth. The creation of the façade is not only important for us to draw fuel; it is a fundamental part of why our smear campaigns are so effective.

The existence of the façade creates a backdrop that means the starting points is that we are to be believed unless there is overwhelming evidence to the contrary. Much like the presumption of innocence with guilt having to be proven, the existence of the façade means we are assumed to be decent, kind and trustworthy until someone is able to prove to the contrary and do so convincingly. Do not under estimate the power of the façade. We invest considerable time and energy in creating and preserving it. We do so for a reason. It serves us particularly well and is perhaps at its most effective in the context of a smear campaign.

It raises the presumption we are right, it proves difficult to shift and it convinces those who might be waverers.

3. You Don't Help Yourself

You fall right into our trap with a lot of your behaviour when you discover that you are being smeared. Rather than consider obtaining some independent and impartial evidence which you present in a calm and measured manner, allowing people to reach their own conclusions, you charge around, wild-eyed and upset, declaring repeatedly that

"It is him, not me, can you not see it? You must be blind or stupid if you cannot."

This will not endear you to anybody. Nobody likes to be criticised. By slating their ability to make a decision you make them defensive and it becomes easier for them to make a decision which favours us. Do they believe the calm individual who has presented as such for the last year or so and who has come to explain you have a problem and we need help to deal with it or do they believed the swivel-eyed, tear-stained, histrionic person who keeps protesting it is not them? It is not a difficult decision to make.

Of course we encourage you to present in such a manner through our steady manipulative treatment of you. Moreover, we know that it mightily offends you to be thought of as something that you are not and in your frazzled and highly-strung state, you will not approach the denial of the smearing in a rationale or constructive fashion. This heightens the effectiveness of what we are doing. To some extent, you are proving our case for us.

4. You Are Eroded

Linked to the above is the fact that when the smear campaign starts you will in all likelihood have been subjected to a sustained period of devaluation which has taken its toll on you. You will be exhausted from our tactics of preventing you from sleeping. You are anxious. You are hypervigilant. You cannot think straight owing to fatigue and the gas lighting to which you have been subjected. Your confidence has been whittled away and your ability to think in a critical fashion has been damaged. The combination of all these ailments means that you are ill-equipped to fight the battle with us for the minds and hearts of those observing. We got in first and you will always be fighting an uphill battle with few resources to rely on. You will have been isolated by us from your support networks. At best this means you cannot call on help when you most need it. At worst this results in those people you thought you could rely on, taking our side. This ineffectiveness of your ability to cope – caused by us – result in our campaign becoming more effective.

5. Aversion to Conflict

People do not like conflict. People hate it when a couple divorces. It is not so much about feeling sad for the fact that two people they like are splitting up. Instead, it is more about the selfishness which means they have to choose on over the other and they would rather not do so. They want people to get along and when we present to those observing that we have tried to make things work but you have not allowed this to happen, the observers' inherent desire for people to get along causes them to prejudge you. You become labelled as the troublemaker. People have their own lives to lead and they want everything else to run smoothly around them. If you are preventing this state of affairs from existing, then this will result in those supposedly impartial observers taking our side and not wanting anything to do with you because you have breached the peace. Knowing this to be the case of course will cause you to react even more and it becomes self-fulfilling. Again, this backdrop of the mind-set of others has this impact on the effectiveness of our campaigns.

People are too busy with their own lives to want to become embroiled in the conflict of others. They do not want the aggravation that it entails as they have concerns and problems of their own. They do not want to have to believe badly of someone that they think well of and they do not want to be seen as inconsistent or wrong. People like to think that are a good judge of character and if it transpires that someone they thought of in good terms is actually not such a good person, it has the potential to make them look and feel stupid. Accordingly, it is far easier to bury their head in the sand and not become involved in the dispute, leaving you, as the victim of the smear campaign, in a difficult position. The audience already think well of us, owing to the façade, it is you who is trying to persuade them to take a different and contrary position. If they will not listen to you. If they will not become involved, how can you persuade them? The odds are stacked against you.

6. Entrenchment

The entrenchment factor must be considered in two respects. Firstly, with regard to the Defective Appliance, Trouble Maker, Predecessor and Primary Source ("the Immediate Effect") and then with regard to the Stigmatised Individual.

In terms of the Immediate Effect concerning these four classes of victims, the smear campaign is unleashed quickly, intensely and driven forward with considerable urgency and energy because the risk increases with each additional person in the audience that the victim will be tipped-off. The smear campaign in this instance gains effectiveness from it being entrenched through its immediacy. It is raw, fresh and "everyone" is talking about it. With so many people talking about, it gains its own traction and becomes entrenched in that sense. The victim, once he or she finds out about the smear campaign may try to quash it and set the record straight but the victim is chasing lots of different agitators and thus their efforts are diminished and spread thin. This dilutes the efficacy of their own efforts and allows the smear campaign to become further entrenched. The speed of the smear campaign's progress and the degree to which it is broadcast creates its own entrenchment which makes it effective.

With respect to the Stigmatised Individual this smear campaign is effective because its entrenchment arises from years of emphasis and reinforcement. It is likely that the audience for this will be smaller than in the case of the Immediate Effect smear campaigns, but those in the audience will have been subjected to the steady and sustained drip drip drip effect meaning that they will have rarely heard anything about the victim other than the ongoing smear campaign. It will be second nature to them and colour their thinking to such a degree that it is massively effective. This smear campaign derives its effectiveness from a slow burn over many years, to a confined audience and the steady accumulation of the untruths against the victim.

7. Acquired Knowledge

We obtain information about our victims when we target them, when we seduce them and when we devalue you them. This information is gathered, refined, stored and used when required and in the most appropriate fashion. Sometimes it will be used to enhance the seduction. Other times it forms the basis of stinging barbs used during devaluation. It may prove the irresistible lure arising from a hoover. This accumulated intelligence which you feely provide to us will also be used during the smear campaign. Knowing what we do about you, in extensive and intimate detail, provides us with plenty of ammunition to use in the following types of smear campaign: -

a. Those where we know something sensitive or embarrassing about you, which is true but was told to us in confidence;

b. Where we are able to use the nugget of truth which you have provided to us and then spun it;

c. We know of something which troubles you and therefore invite lies to use in the smear campaign based on that vulnerability.

Having access to all of this information about you ensures that when the smear campaign is commenced it is far more effective.

What Effect Does the Smear Campaign Have On Others?

When I refer to others I mean those who form the third part of the parties necessary for a smear campaign to function. There needs to be us as the instigator, you as the target or victim (whether defective appliance, trouble maker, predecessor or primary source) and the final part are the audience, the people who are fed the content of the smear campaign. These people form the recipients of the information but naturally they are not smeared themselves. They are told the truth about your sensitive information, the exaggerated truth or just complete untruths. They are fed a stream of material in order to discredit you and influence their attitudes and views. Before addressing the actual effect that the smear campaign has on its audience it is worth considering who forms this audience.

At its most basic this includes anybody and everybody. If there is a viable link between you, me and them, they will be included. Whilst we are an effective propaganda machine and we are able to rely on our supporters to carry and disseminate the content of the smear campaign for us, we are not a media organisation and therefore it is not the case that the smear campaign will be bulletin news and plastered across the front pages. Whilst we would not rule out some wider media circulation of the smear campaign, that is unusual (this is discussed further in a chapter below). The immediate aim of the smear campaign is to affect certain groups of people first. This is as follows: -

Our Lieutenants

Turncoat Lieutenants

Our Coterie

Turncoat Coterie

(If not part of the above groups)

Our family

Our inner and outer circle friends

Our neighbours

Our colleagues

Yours family

Your inner and outer circle friends

Your neighbours (if different)

Your colleagues

Mutual acquaintances

Mutual minions

Other

It is necessary to keep this order of dissemination in your mind as I explain the effect that a smear campaign has on the audience to it. I will address the various categories above by reference to the effect and this will also touch on why the described order is as it is. There are two stages to consider when addressing the effects of the smear campaign. There is the Audience Receipt, namely the provision of the content of the smear campaign to the relevant groups. Then there follows the Audience Reaction, when the victim becomes aware that they are being smeared. To understand who falls into each of these categories (where it is not obvious from the description alone) you should have regard to the chapter below **"Who Is Involved in the Smear?"**

1. Our Lieutenants/Turncoat Lieutenants

Audience Receipt

The people in these groups are automatically set to receive and obey. These people will not question the content of the smear campaign. There will be no need to persuade them. A simple explanation of the nature of the smear campaign and the instruction to "pass it on" will be sufficient. The quicker these highly loyal people are appraised of the smear campaign the further it will reach and the more effective it will be. These people can be relied on to disseminate the content of the smear campaign, in the most effective fashion and also be able to persuade people of the content of the smear. It is as if these people are chanting a mantra, propagating the same message to all those that they are instructed to tell. These two groups will be given clear instructions as to who they are to tell in order to ensure maximum dissemination, maximum effectiveness and reduce the risk of tip-off to the victim. These groups will believe the content of the smear without question. They will continue to deal with the victim to the extent it is necessary but will look to minimise their involvement with that person, for example reneging on an existing arrangement, not returning calls, not answering messages and so forth. There is no risk they will tip the victim off.

Audience Reaction

Once the victim becomes aware of the smear campaign and approaches these groups they will allow the victim to approach them but they will offer no assistance and will prevent any attempt to persuade them to adopt a contrary view. Indeed, they will repeat the smear to the victim in order to further their upset, anger and/or frustration for the purposes of maintaining the smear and drawing fuel for our benefit.

2. Our Coterie/ Turncoat Coterie

Audience Receipt

Similar to the lieutenants these are also loyal groups. They will receive the content of the smear campaign and will not question it. They will be instructed to keep the information to themselves for the time being. This is to prevent any leaks. They will comply with this instruction. They will believe what they are being told and will not challenge it. They will also minimise their involvement with the victim so far as they are able using plausible grounds.

Audience Reaction

Once the victim is aware, the members of these groups will also engage with the victim but they will offer no assistance and they will not be persuaded to the contrary. They are unlikely to keep maintaining the smear in the same aggressive manner as the lieutenants but they will believe it and they will not look to alter their stance.

There is a threshold that is applicable beyond these groups. After this the risk of a leak to the victim is greater and therefore it is necessary for us as the instigator to move with due haste to disseminate the information as widely as possible so it can sink in and take effect before the victim learns and is able to respond.

3. Our family

Audience Receipt

They will accept the information and believe it, backing us and providing us with support. They will minimise their interaction with the victim as far as possible.

Audience Reaction

They will allow the victim an audience in some instances and in others this will be refused. They will state our case to the victim and whilst sounding sympathetic to the comments of the victim they will not be persuaded unless there is overwhelming evidence which destroys our position. They will not turn their backs on the victim but rather suggest ways they might help themselves to overcome the problems which are the nature of the smear, change their ways and mend their behaviour in order to possibly save the relationship. They will not suggest that we have done anything wrong or that we need to change our behaviours in any way.

4. Our inner and outer circle friends

The likelihood is that most of these people will be in our coterie although there may be one or two exceptions. They will be told in the expectation of co-operation.

Audience Receipt

They will believe the information provided and will not challenge it. They are unlikely to alter this view unless there is overwhelming information to the contrary. They will spread the smear as part of gossiping but will not be in any rush to do so and will not do so with the haste of the lieutenants or the coterie (once so instructed).

Audience Reaction

They will turn their backs on the victim.

5. Our Neighbours

Audience Receipt

They will react with surprise at the information but accept it. They will only have their minds altered by overwhelming evidence. They will disseminate the information but only to other neighbours.

Audience Reaction

They will speak to the victim if the victim is persistent and allow them to state their case out of politeness but unless there is overwhelming evidence they will remain unmoved. They are unlikely to offer an assistance to the victim preferring to stay out of the dispute.

6. Our colleagues

Audience Receipt

They will accept what they are told. They are unlikely to tip off the victim owing to the fact they may know them vaguely or know of them. Their loyalty to us in terms of job position and the need to get on with us will outweigh any desire to tip the victim off. They will disseminate the information with other colleagues.

Audience Reaction

They will refuse an audience preferring not to get involved and will turn their backs on the victim.

It should be noted that a further threshold is crossed at this point as the smear is rolled out to people that you know better than us, who are likely to have greater loyalty to you and thus the risk of tip-off increases considerably.

7. Your family

Audience Receipt

They will be surprised and disappointed to learn of the content of the smear. They will try to approach it in a constructive fashion, ascertaining if there is anything they can do to help both parties. They will tell the victim even if asked not to.

Audience Reaction

There will be a period of paralysis as they are torn between their shock and dismay at learning that the relationship has ended and also the reason for that resting with the behaviour of their relative. Some relations will remain disappointed and try to form a constructive view. Others will place their head in the sand and expect you and I to sort it out ourselves (note the damage has already been done despite you stating your case). Others will rally to the assistance of the smeared victim but the prospects of this happening have been reduced by the smear.

Note that anybody who is a family member who will turn their back on the victim will be included as a Turncoat Lieutenant or Turncoat Coterie. This point is applicable to all classes of supporter who are regarded as being in your camp.

8. Your inner and outer circle friends

Audience Receipt

The information will be received but these people will be undecided and will want to hear the victim's side of the story as well before making a determination. There is a high risk of the victim being tipped off and it is not expected to necessarily cause this class of supporter to turn against the victim but rather sow doubt in their minds, thus delaying the provision of any assistance to the victim.

Audience Reaction

This group is likely to be persuaded to assist the victim, although there is always potential for them to want to remain out of the conflict. They are not going to assist our cause otherwise they would have been recruited as a turncoat.

9. Your neighbours

Audience Receipt

They will receive the information and are unlikely to argue against it, preferring to remain out of the dispute.

Audience Reaction

The victim will plead their case but unless the neighbour falls into the category of being the victim's friend, the neighbours will keep out of the dispute.

10. Your colleagues

Audience Receipt

There is likely to be concerns raised which will result in the victim being asked about the nature of the smears if they impact on the victim's capability to undertake their job.

Audience Reaction

The victim may persuade their colleagues that there is nothing to be concerned about although most will not want to get involved if it does not impact on the person's job.

Mutual Acquaintances/Minions/Other

With both receipt and reaction, the usual reaction from these groups is to withdraw from involvement with either party and not become involved.

These responses are based on what I have witnessed when I have instigated a smear campaign. There will always be exceptions, working both ways, but in the majority of instances these are the reactions from people when first told the nature of the smear and how they respond once the victim is aware of what is being said and tries to set the record straight in some way. Do not discount the cumulative effect of the smear. In certain instances, especially tight-knit groups and smaller communities, the effect can be exacerbated so that the majority opinion is such so that your supporters becomes "infected" by this so that those that might help, stay out of the dispute and those that might stay out of it, turn their backs on you and have nothing more to do with you.

You will note that amongst our Lieutenants, Coterie and Turncoats only out smear will prevail and the victim will find cold comfort with those people. That is why it is important to recruit as many people as we can into these categories to maximise the prospect of the smear being successful and to have significant impact against you. The balance of our supporters may listen to you but you will find no help and will either face people turning their backs on you or not wanting to be involved. Those people who would be regarded as in your camp and who have not proven to be turncoats will be those who may continue to support you. The best we will achieve is to cause people to not want to get involved and to sow some seeds of doubt which cause distress to you when you are questioned by your own supporters as to what you have supposedly done. The effect on people will either be: -

a. They support us and actively propagate the smear;
b. They support us and deny your counter-allegations;
c. They turn their backs on you and offer no support or assistance;
d. They do not want to get involved

e. They support you but at a minimal level, remaining concerned by what has been spread around about you;

f. They reject the smear and provide you with support and assistance.

Certain additional factors (cumulative effect, nature of the campaign, number of lieutenants, nature of community in which it takes places) can magnify the effect so that it becomes better for us and worse for you than usual.

The advantage we have is that the speed at which we move and the fact we "get in first" means we have the chance to cause considerable damage to you and reduce those who you might rely on. There is also the fact that people tend to believe what they are told, people enjoy gossip, people revel in the misfortune of others and people are too wrapped up in their own lives to care to do anything. Those additional factors mean that being first carries even more weight. As is often the case mud sticks because people adopt a "no smoke without fire" mentality. Your reputation can be annihilated in a matter of moments and it will take considerable effort on your part. People also will regard repeating protestation on your part with suspicion – she doth protest too much - and whilst they may not say it to your face they will be thinking that the smear is true and thus they are taken in by it.

The fact we are able to get our strike in first and to do so for a period of hours and possibly days before you retaliate and try to counter it, means the damage is often done and the minds of people are made up rather quickly and finally, no matter what you try to do. It certainly appears unfair but the methodology of our smear campaigns relies on: -

- The inherent prejudice of people
- The speed by which people judge
- Their capacity to believe what they are told
- The use of plausibility to drive home a convincing truth
- People thinking in predictable and regimented ways which we are able to exploit

All of this means that the smear campaign is weighted heavily in our favour and the audience usually biased towards you and remains that way, despite your best efforts. All you may be able to do is ameliorate the effects a little and those effects on you are detailed further below.

It should be noted that the effect will be somewhat different where the smear campaign is in respect of a Stigmatised Individual. In such an instance the following are more likely to apply: -

- The smear will last far longer;
- The audience will be limited to lieutenants and coterie drawn from the family, plus other family members with only a handful of others involved (close inner circle friends of ours, a teacher, a doctor)

- The recipients will almost without question accept the nature of the smear because of its insidious nature, the fact the victim will not know about it for a long time, the fact the victim is a child as is largely ignored since "the adults know better" and its repeated reinforcement. Added to this is the fact that much of this type of smear campaign will be done under the auspices of Fake Concern, which is expanded on in respect of the types of smear campaign below.
- The audience will always side with the narcissist and offer assistance, regarding the victim as in need of help (although the victim may not know why when he or she was child) and later they will be regarded as beyond assistance, having rejected the offered help or failed to comply with it.
- The victim faces an almost impossible task of overturning the nature of the smear campaign in this instance.

What Effect Does the Smear Campaign Have On You?

The ultimate purpose of the smear campaign is the effect that it has on you. Smear campaigns are a constant in the arsenal of the narcissist. Effective, utilised most often through word of mouth and with the capacity to envelop many people at once who in turn perpetuate the smear, the smear campaign is a favoured manipulation of our kind.

1. Denial of assistance

The smear campaign is usually utilised during devaluation and on the cusp of discard when dealing with a primary source victim. If used against you as a predecessor, you will still be reeling from the discard, the rejection of your attempts to get back with us or the pressure of sustaining no contact if you chose that avenue. Its timing is such that you will more likely than not find yourself in a position of desperation, fatigue and confusion. Battered and buffeted by our manipulations through the devaluation period, you are in a poor position to defend yourself never mind having to defend your reputation with others. Once the discard hits you and knocks you for six, you are in need of considerable assistance. You need somebody to help you make sense of what has just happened. You need somebody to listen to you as you pore over the relationship and try to piece together (usually unsuccessfully) the cause of your fall from grace and subsequent discard. You will need assistance on practical items such as money, paying bills, eating, child care, washing and cleaning in some of the more extreme cases where your ability to function has been hammered. When your need for external assistance is at its highest, you find that those who you thought you could rely on to help you have been poisoned. Those who were amongst our supporters initially will not provide you with any help, no matter how desperate you are. Friends become unobtainable or suddenly busy with other commitments. Family are sceptical about helping you since they think you have brought it on yourself and they are even ashamed of your supposed behaviour. Those of your supporters who have become Turncoats will not only fail to help you but their shunning of you will hurt all the more. Colleagues are not inclined to assist someone who has been painted the way you have. These people disappear, turn their backs or even worse ally with our kind and the help and assistance you so desperately need has been taken away from you. This furthers your isolation, your pain and your distress. It also reduces your capability to address the nature of the smear campaign and neutralise it.

This denial of assistance from people you thought would help you, both amongst our supporters and your own is tantamount to kicking you when you are down.

2. The Corruption of the Truth

You abide by the truth. You speak it and live by it. Yes, you may tell the odd white lie but you are a paragon of virtue compared to our mendacious and repeated untruths. You believe in the truth and you need others to know that you are an honest and truthful person. You base your life on having honest dealing with people, both towards them and from them. It has been an horrendous enough experience dealing with our lies that we told time and time again to you, but it becomes even worse when you are being lied about. You may have reached the conclusion that we are well-practised liars and that is the way we are but to have your own reputation impugned and your character stained as a liar is anathema to you. This causes distress and the fact you know that other people are believing a lie about you will have a damaging effect on you and we know this full well.

The fact that people you once trusted, both in our camp and especially your own, believe this corrupted truth becomes all the more painful. Add to this that those same people are continuing to provide energy to the smear campaign by believing it and spreading the content further and the hurt increases. You should also be aware that those people who are in our coterie and who are our Lieutenants will actually be getting a kick out of your distress at this corrupted truth. They feel superior by knowing something about you, something which hurts you and they are perfectly happy to keep repeating it and see you wounded by it. They have been infected with our way of thinking and they are pleased that they are on our team, the winning team and not yours. Not only do they believe the smear campaign and spread it, they also pour scorn on you for this behaviour. Others may turn their backs on you and refuse to help, but you see this corrupted truth being flung in your face by people who are no better than you, who are now sitting in moral judgement of you.

3. Frustration

You feel a huge sense of frustration that your reputation is being smeared but added to that is the frustration that people are actually believing what is being said about you. You are surprised and dismayed that people are falling for what we are saying about you. You are disappointed in those people who you thought would know better than to be taken in by what we have said. You really ought to know by now that just as you were taken in by our charm and seduction, so have they. Did you really expect them to respond any differently when you did not? The difficulty is, is that you know the truth about the lies being spun about you and you desperately want others to see through this but they do not. You understand why, because we base the smear on a grain of truth, we magnify and manipulate and twist and warp the truth so that people are deceived in an expert fashion but nevertheless you really though that people who you could rely on would see through this tissue of lies, this web of deceit. The frustration at this overwhelms you and adds to the distress of the situation as a whole.

Try as you might to dislodge the nature of the smear campaign, it has become too ingrained, too reinforced and has acquired its own energy so that there are too many people all taking the same view. This majority power proves to be a tidal wave which you cannot stop or turn back and instead it swamps you. This feeling of powerlessness will add to your frustration and make a difficult situation feel even worse.

4. The Lack of Control

We hate losing control. Most people do not like to lose control because this causes distress, anxiety and apprehension. If something bad happens and you are able to at least do something to address it, counter it or mitigate its effect you automatically feel better. However, if you are swept along on a tide by a force over which you can exert no control, the sense of helplessness is massive. You are made to feel like this because when the smear campaign commences your coping ability has been hugely reduced. We however are at the top of our game, calling the shots and orchestrating everything with considerable effectiveness. You do not truly understand why it is happening, why we are behaving like this and moreover why people believe what we are saying. You feel as if you have no control over the progression and outcome of the smear campaign and this increases its effectiveness in terms of how it affects you.

Being an honest and decent person, your immediate reaction to a smear campaign is usually to try to correct it and set the record straight. It is an understandable and laudable sentiment and it is one which we rely on you trying to achieve because you will be on a hiding to nothing. Too many people know, too many people have adopted an entrenched attitude (especially those which are coterie members and Lieutenants and we will look to increase those numbers ahead of a smear campaign) and therefore you are left fire-fighting. Add this to your general anxiety, fatigue and hurt, this additional sense of being unable to do anything to stop this false and unfair smear campaign is devastating. When we feel we have no control over a situation it magnifies all sensations of worry, anxiety, concern and such like. By the time you realise that a smear campaign has been used against you then it is invariably too late to do anything. The audience is wide and they have had the smear reinforced so that they are unlikely to believe what you say and even if they did, they would not necessarily want to lose face by changing their opinion. In such an instance it is easier for them to reject you and turn their backs.

5. Keeping Up Appearances

Related to the corruption of the truth. Whereas the corruption of the truth alarms you because of the way that a central quality which you adhere to and believe in is being damaged, the smear campaign is also damaging how people think about you. You are not a person who is immersed in pride. You are neither vain nor conceited but you still want people to think well of you because you are a good and decent person. You just want people to know what you are and to have them told that you are something contrary to your actual appearance becomes especially upsetting for you.

6. The Hammer to Your Reputation

Not only is your character and outward appearance as a good and honest person shattered and dented by the smear campaign, the effects of a smear campaign often go further. Your professional integrity is called into question with ramifications for your job, career advancement and livelihood. Your standing in the community is adversely affected which could have repercussions where you hold positions of trust and authority. If you have to be licensed by the authorities in some way, a smear campaign can place that in jeopardy. You may lose friends, your family may distance themselves from you but the repercussions of a smear campaign can infect your professional life, your income, your integrity and your standing. You are made to feel like a pariah and you may lose clients and customers, the backing of your superiors, be regarded as an albatross to an organisation. People are obsessed with appearances and if you become a PR nightmare not only is your personal life hammered by the smear campaign your professional and business standing is also.

7. Increased susceptibility to hoover

The horrible nature of the smear campaign, the anxiety, hurt and isolation that it causes means that victim will have a difficult time dealing with it. If the victim has also suffered a savage devaluation and callous discard, then the cumulative effect will be considerable. They may have felt that they have been chasing ghosts when dealing with those smear campaigns which rely on the Immediacy Effect (Defective Appliance, Trouble Maker, Predecessor and Primary Source Victims) or that they are dealing with an immovable force where the smear takes the form of stigmatisation. Worn down, troubled, unheard and unbelieved the victim will be offered a way of ending the smear campaign and thus halting the hurt. We will hoover the victim and do so in a benign manner. We can easily distance ourselves from the nature of the smear campaign because:
-

- They are usually word of mouth, therefore there is always doubt as to what has been said;
- Our lack of accountability enables us to effect this without concern;
- Our ability to blame others and the fact that others were involved in smearing you means we can pin the blame on other people;
- We will, where there is evidence linking us to the smear campaign which is credible, brush over it, admit a mistake or explain we were hurt, angry etc.;
- You desire for relief will take precedence over apportioning blame.

Accordingly, the fact that we are behind the smear campaign will not stand in the way at all in terms of bringing you back to us. The charm exemplified in this hoover combined with the miserable state you find yourself in means that you are at considerable risk of being hoovered by us. The smear campaign is used to soften you up for this additional manipulation. More often than not you will fall for the hoover because: -

- It will halt the smear campaign;
- You hope to receive some answers as to why it happened (you will not)
- Your resistance is low;
- There will be pressure from our supporters for you to accept (instigated by us) but also from your supporters (they want an end to the smear campaign for everyone's sakes and also because they want a peaceful existence).

8. Distress

The nature of the smear campaigns will vary (see below) but at the heart of them all is the fact that they rely on fear and distress to make them effective. Nobody likes untruths to be told about them. Nobody likes to hear those untruths appertain to nasty, demeaning and sensitive matters. Nobody wants to hear them said to them and even less for other people to hear them and then believe them. Facing many people who have been infected with the smear campaign, who either turn their back on you, repeat the allegations or chastise you means that the effect of a smear campaign will be distressing. It will cause anxiety, it will affect your ability to sleep, it will affect your decision-making skills, appetite and ability to function. In certain instances, the breadth of the campaign, along with the vicious nature of it can cause serious and long-lasting effects to the well-being of an individual all airings from the distress that has been caused.

9. Utilisation of required resources

A further effect of the smear campaign is that is causes you to utilise your resources which would be better spent looking after yourself and others dependent on your care. The time spent worrying, investigating and trying to persuade people (the latter often done in an ineffective manner) means that you are wasting time which would be better utilised to protecting yourself, applying no contact, rallying those people you can trust to assist you and taking care of yourself and your life. It is typical of our manipulation of you that we like to open up several fronts against you so that you struggle to cope with this onslaught. Added to this that in certain instances (usually the Primary Source and Predecessor Victims situations) your resources will already be stretched thin. By making you address the smear campaign we are causing you to divert resources which you could apply elsewhere. This in turn reduces your ability to fight the smear campaign and means you remain susceptible to the hoover which will bring it to an end but on our terms.

10.Acceptance

This can happen in respect of the Immediate Effect smear campaigns (usually the Primary Source and Predecessor Victim situations) when the victim, having been subjected to the debilitating effects of devaluation, discard and now smear campaign have their self-confidence, self-esteem and critical thinking capabilities eroded to such a degree that they actually accept that the content of the smear campaign is true in whole or in part. They will blame themselves and consider that they deserved to be treated in this way. In actual fact this is a way for the victim to protect him or herself. Unable to fight any longer and without resources to reject the smear campaign, they give in and accept it must be right in part or in whole and therefore this will alleviate them from trying to use resources to counter it. In this state the victim will remain vulnerable to being hoovered but they are less likely to provide fuel since they will no longer be reacting (or reacting as greatly) to the smear campaign. They will allow it to burn itself out as they hide away from it. They may experience some effects of it still but by giving up they actually will lessen some of the impact, but remain exposed to a hoover.

The acceptance is particularly pronounced with regard to a smear campaign which is used to stigmatise an individual. This person will not actually "give up" and accept it but believe this to be the truth of who they are because so many people believe it and reinforce it. They will say to themselves,

"If so many other people say it of me, perhaps they are right and I am wrong?"

This will mean that the victim may find their self-esteem plummeting and they will find themselves particularly vulnerable to the control of the narcissist who has implanted this idea. This is because the victim will look to the narcissist (who is the architect of this smear) for answers and perversely for guidance as to how they may improve themselves. They may even seek forgiveness and absolution from the narcissist which of course is something the narcissist will delight in, in terms of fuel and the reinforcement of his or her power.

Who is involved in the smear campaign?

Whilst we consider ourselves omnipotent, mighty and all-conquering it remains the fact that we are unable to do much of what is required to gather our fuel, execute our machinations and exert control without the assistance of our supporters. Gaining supporters is important to us and it is not difficult for us to do so. Much in the same way that we seduce the person who we install as a primary source of fuel, we seduce people to become our supporters. What does it take to become one of our supporters? You must provide fuel, that is paramount and something that we expect from all those who we recruit to be our supporters. Predictably enough however we want more than just fuel. We want your obedience, we want you to speak well of us to others and accept our views over those advanced by other people. We want you to provide us with character traits which we can purloin for ourselves and pass them off as our own to the rest of the world. We want you to carry out our orders. Not everybody that we recruit is able to carry out these requirements and therefore this results in us having different classifications of supporter. These supporters are also of paramount importance in respect of the instigation of the smear campaign because without an audience and a willing one at that, the smear campaign will fail. In the context of a smear campaign, these supporters are needed for the following reasons: -

- To believe the smear campaign
- To provide us with fuel when reacting to the smear campaign;
- To assist in spreading the smear campaign;
- To create the Majority Effect by having more and more people accept the content of the smear campaign it gains traction and thus reaches more people who are even more likely to accept it;
- To cause hurt to the victim by snubbing them, questioning them and/or chastising them for their supposed behaviour;

Accordingly, the role of the audience in a smear campaign is very important. This also means that we want the audience to be on our side, proactive and believing, amenable to our lies and against the victim. The audience comprises of four main groups of people: -

Our supporters (our camp)

Your supporters (your camp)

Mutual supporters

Non-supporters (e.g. minions, strangers)

Where do these supporters come from? When you first become entangled with our kind you will notice that we have family, friends, colleagues and acquaintances who think highly of us. There will be occasions when someone who appears to be a stranger will stop and say hello to us on the street. We receive particularly good service from a waitress who evidently knows who we are. Our supporters are drawn from everybody around us. They do not all have to be friends with us, many supporters remain in the ranks of acquaintances, colleagues and minions without ever advancing to the status of being an inner or outer circle friend, but for every category of proximity of supply of fuel that exists, those people are our supporters. There will be an impressive infrastructure of supporters in place when we first interact but it will not end there. We want your supporters to become our supporters. Of course, those who support you are your supporters for completely different reasons to our supporters. That does not matter. Your supporters will also be subjected to the charm, pleasantness, kindness and magnetism in order to draw them into our sphere of influence and anoint them as one of our supporters and to place them into the relevant category. We regard it as fundamental that we recruit your supporters to be ours. At first it is not a mutually exclusive arrangement. Indeed, since you are firmly in the golden period then it is easy for these people to support you and I. It is once the devaluation begins and especially when a smear campaign is launched that the value of your supporters to us becomes greater. It is then that those supporters show their true worth to my kind by altering the way that they deal with you and/or refusing to alter the way that they deal with us. We always aim to recruit from your ranks.

So, what are the categories that we classify these supporters into?

1. Drawn from Our Supporters

The Façade – I regularly make mention of how the maintenance of the façade is important. We want the world to think we are kind, wonderful, interesting, charming, generous and an all-round decent person. Those people who are assigned to the façade provide us with fuel and think well of us. The façade is supported by a cast array of people ranging from family, friends, colleagues all the way through to strangers. We want all your supporters to buy into this as well, as a minimum, so that when the time comes to devalue you, smear you and discard you, you find that you run into a wall of unimpeachable individuals who all believe that we would never hurt you, that we are decent and you must be making it up, exaggerating or taking things out of proportion.

The Reverse Façade – this is applicable to those who are Stigmatised Individuals. Whilst there is a façade which means we are well-regarded, the creation of the reverse façade means that the victim becomes regarded in a poor light by the audience.

The Coterie – this is our stable of highly visible supporters. They can be relied on to provide us with fuel, more often and to a greater degree than those who are in the façade. This group will contain people who can provide us with those character traits which we like to steal. They believe everything that we say and are very difficult to persuade that the façade is just an illusion. They will gladly do things for us but are not engaged to directly carry out our machinations against you. We do not regard their loyalty and blind obedience to be that great. However, if we ask them to tell the world how great we are, they will do so. If we want to borrow money, get a lift somewhere, have them pick up a parcel and so forth they will willingly do so. The coterie is a competitive place where its members vie against one another for our favour, in order to show that they get to spend longer with us, or time with us alone, or that we have praised them over someone else. The coterie can be relied on to always agree with us, disagree with you, laugh at our jokes, stand and listen to our anecdotes and marvel at our magnificence. The coterie will embrace you warmly when we begin our seduction of you but do not be fooled. None of them like you. They only pretend to do so in order to gain our favour. They are jealous because they want to be our favourite, they want to be the primary source. They do not know what a primary source is, in the same way that you don't, but they want to be regarded in the same way as the way we regard you during the seduction. This promise of a more intense golden period to the one that they already enjoy keeps them in line. Imagine a royal court and these courtiers are always to hand, gossiping, scheming and pretending in order to gain some royal grace and favour from their monarch; us. When we give the signal this group of people will turn their backs on you, happily disseminate our propaganda about you and support our smearing of you.

Turncoat Coterie – this group is as the above Coterie but contains those people who were once your supporters. Initially the person is admitted to our coterie because they are content to support both you and I and during the golden period there is no difficulty. This person has been earmarked for the Turncoat Coterie because they naturally promote the façade but they want more. They often contact us and not you, they talk to us without you being around and as time progresses we ensure that their loyalty to us becomes greater than their loyalty to you. To put it in your parlance, they start off as one of your friends, become both our friends and then decide they want to be my friend rather than remain friends with you. This person's status is never apparent until it is time for them to make a choice between you and I, which is usually around the time of a smear campaign and discard. They will not actively do anything against you, but they will promote our smear to others and turn their back on you when we decree that ought to be done. Not only do we revel in such a recruitment since it bolsters the number of our supporters, but it also means that you will be hurt by their treachery and this provides us with fuel and emphasises our power.

Lieutenants – the agents who believe what we say, remain loyal and will carry out our demands in order to retain our favour and receive other tokens of our appreciation and largesse. Our lieutenants are not only those who will provide us with fuel, carry out favours for us but they will actively assist us in our machinations. Whether it is finding out information about a prospective target before we engage, administering one of our devaluing manipulations by proxy or utilising the lieutenant in a hoover, these are the elite of our supporters. They may not number many in nature and they do not know what we are, other than they regard us as a brilliant and magnetic person who has also done right by them. We will have undertaken favours for them in order to secure their loyalty. We will also have some "dirt" on them as well which we will use to apply pressure if we have any concerns that their loyalty is wavering. The Lieutenant can be called on for fuel in times of emergency, to assist us in our smear campaigns, to gather information for us and to remain loyal. I like to keep one lieutenant that you do not know about so that he or she can be used with impunity often during a hoover. Unaware that this person is connected to me, your defences will be lowered and this will enable my lieutenant to acquire information from you and initiate contact for me to improve the prospects of the hoover succeeding. You may find that not long after you have escaped us that you are approached by someone who seems interested in you romantically. There is a good chance this person is a hitherto unknown Lieutenant of ours. Not only does this improve the hoover prospects but if you happen to succumb to it and later escape or evade it in the first place and realise that a Lieutenant was involved, this will cause you to remain anxious about anybody else who engages with your romantically. This causes you to struggle to move forward and find someone new who will distract you from thinking about us.

Turncoat Lieutenant - the ultimate supporter. This person is a friend or family member of yours who you think that you can rely on and trust, but in actual fact they are loyal to me and not only that they are actively briefing against you. It is this person who enables me to acquire your new mobile telephone number after you have changed it post escape. It is this person who tells me where you have moved to, where you will be on a particular evening and who you are fraternising with in order to maximise my attempt to hoover you. This person will operate on our behalf so that during devaluation when you are seeking solace from them and trying to understand what is happening this Turncoat Lieutenant will be advancing reasons which support my position and undermine yours. You can expect them to tell you.

"Are you sure that is what really happened?"

"I think you are over-reacting to be honest."

"Maybe if you tired x or y, he may calm down."

"Well, is it any wonder, he works really hard, he is probably stressed."

"That's not something to worry about, trust me."

"You are becoming fixated with something that isn't a problem."

"He does a lot for you you know, often you don't know about it."

"I find that hard to believe, he is always fine with me."

"He wouldn't mean that. I think you are seeing something which isn't there."

"Take it from me, I know he has your best interests at heart."

If you start hearing comments which sound as if they could be uttered by my kind, you are most likely dealing with a Turncoat Lieutenant. Often this individual has fallen for the lies we have told about you and the charm we have sent in their direction. If this person is of the opposite sex (or same if we are of that particular sexual orientation) there is a good chance they are your replacement and the reward for their loyalty to us and betrayal of you, will be to replace you as our primary source and as our intimate partner. This person will advance any smears against you and also persuade others amongst your supporters that we are right and you are wrong, causing confusion and doubt. Their impact is significant and we always aim to recruit such a person. They will often remain undetected, waiting for when we need to activate them and then they will cause havoc in your camp, undermining you to others, turning people against you and having you doubt yourself. A Turncoat Lieutenant is a dangerous weapon once recruited by us.

These categories are the most loyal of our supporters. We do however draw supporters who may not be part of the coterie (turncoat or otherwise) or lieutenants (turncoat or otherwise) from our friends, family, colleagues as well as acquaintances, minions and even strangers in some instances. We aim in a smear campaign to maximise the number of supporters that we have so the smear spread far and quickly, creating a Majority Effect and overwhelming you when you eventually find out.

Of course those who are our supporters are the ones which are of the greatest importance to our smear campaign but there are others who are involved.

2. Your Supporters

We will recruit Turncoats and thereafter still look to influence your supporters. We will cause them to doubt you, not want to get involved and whist we may not be able to recruit them to our camp so they turn against you, we want to disrupt as much as possible those who might provide you with some assistance once you learn about the smear campaign. We allow the smear campaign to reach your supporters later because whilst it is important for them to be involved, their involvement brings with it an increased risk of you being tipped-off and potentially assisted.

3. Mutual Supporters

There will also be those people who cannot be regarded as belonging to either camp. We want them involved in the smear campaign because whilst they may not help us, we do not want them helping you either. Accordingly, the aim with this group is to neutralise them so that they decide to stay out of the conflict altogether. This suits us because we have already made sure that we have plenty of supporters so the loss of assistance amongst these mutual supporters does not have that great an effect on us. It will of course have a greater impact on you because the pot from which you can draw support is far smaller.

4. Non-supporters

These people tend to be drawn from strangers, minions and acquaintances and would not be regarded as wanting to assist either party. We will be content for the smear to reach them as well in order to prevent them assisting you and/or causing them to assist us. We will not expend much energy however in ensuring that these people are affected.

5. You as Primary Source

There is a fifth grouping that becomes involved in the audience of the smear campaign and that is you when you are the primary source. You are part of the audience when we smear: -

- A Defective Appliance;
- A Trouble Maker;
- A Predecessor
- A Stigmatised Individual

You are expected to believe everything we say in these smear campaigns. Your total loyalty is also expected and demanded because you actually often play an important part in these smear campaigns. Once the victim knows about the smear campaign it is likely that they will try to confront us to persuade us to stop, set the record straight and even just to attack us for what we have done. Since you are the primary source you spend more time with us than most and therefore if such a confrontation arises then you have an important role to play in witnessing the unnecessary attack. We can then rely on your recollection of it to reinforce the smear campaign further as you tell people how unreasonable the victim behaved, how unhinged they are, how they will not leave us alone and so on and so forth. This means that this creates added credibility to our smear campaign, it rejuvenates it and causes the victim added hurt.

In addition, the victim may not confront us and instead try to get to us through you since after all you are our intimate partner and perhaps if you can be persuaded to accept the victim's position then you can bring persuasion to bear against us also?

In such a situation we are content for you to allow the victim an audience but if you do not and you reject them out of hand we are pleased with that reaction. If you do listen to them, you will more than likely reject what they have to say because: -

- We have brainwashed you into accepting our version of events way ahead of the victim being aware of what is going on and being able to counter it;

- You do not want to lose us. You remain in the golden period and we can do no wrong. Therefore, on balance you will accept our version. You also do not want to believe what the other person is saying (even if it may appear true) for fear of having the golden image you have of us shattered.

Thus we are relaxed about this person approaching you because we know that most of the time you will reject what they are saying and advance our position so that the victim yields more fuel and becomes even more desperate.

You ought to pay heed that if you are witnessing our denigration and smearing of people who were once regarded as friends, lovers and such like you are seeing what will in the fullness of time happen to you.

How is the Smear Campaign Effected?

I detail in the next chapter an array of specific smear campaigns to enable you to know what to expect and to be able to recognise them, but before that is embraced it is worth understanding how the smear campaign is effected. You know that it is a campaign to discredit. You understand when and why it used by us and why it is so effective. You also now understand what the reaction of those in the audience is and what the effect is on the various classes of victims, but how do we go about it?

The first and foremost consideration of any smear campaign is not actually the content. We have so much to choose from in terms of the release of sensitive material and the exaggeration of truths, but even if we did not, we would just make something up. Accordingly, it is not the subject matter which is the primary concern. Of course it requires plausibility and we have due regard to it, but of overall importance is the speed at which the smear is unrolled across the waiting audience.

Once we have decided that a smear campaign is to be used we want it deployed quickly and for it to spread like wildfire. This means that our lieutenants are always told first and they are then instructed to spread the news in accordance with our instructions and to keep doing it. The coterie is involved and we may well have twenty to thirty people involved in propagating the smear at this very early stage. With each of these people spreading the news to say five people, which is easily achievable in just an hour, some 100-150 people are "infected" with the smear campaign in a short space of time.

This is usually done through word of mouth and by telephone. The seeds of the smear campaign will be planted with the lieutenants. The reason for doing it through word of mouth from us provides us with deniability at a later stage if we decide to hoover you and blame the smear campaign on someone else instead. If technology is to be used – through text messages and posts through social media, we leave it to others to do that. They can deal with any subsequent repercussions which may arise if the victim challenges them or escalates the matter further. We may be suspected as being the originator of the smear campaign but it will be difficult to prove that it came from us. It will be suspicion and speculation and we are content to lurk amongst those amorphous and shadowy concepts.

Where we wish to plant a Smear Bomb we will often attend to it ourselves. A Smear Bomb is where there is a particularly serious repercussion which will arise from the particular recipient being provided with the information that forms the smear campaign. An example would be telephoning your employer to advise them you are being investigated for fraud. If you hold a position of trust, the provision of such information will cause considerable repercussions for you, as if a bomb had just gone off. We prefer to attend to his ourselves to ensure that there is maximum effectiveness, that any resistance this person may exhibit (since your employer or someone in authority is unlikely to be in our camp) can be overcome through our persuasive manner and careful release of facts or manipulation of the same. We will take steps to ensure that as detonator of this bomb we are not recognised whilst setting it off so the effect for you is considerable.

The stigmatisation of an individual is done is a subtle and slow-burning fashion. This is not the case with other forms of smear campaign. There is always a risk that you will find and be tipped off. We need the smear campaign to have gained traction and have had considerable effect by the time you learn about it. You will always find out about it and indeed this knowledge is something we rely on in terms of its effectiveness but in order to increase its efficacy we need to have it embedded in the minds of key people quickly so that it fans outwards affecting other people, creating the Majority Effect and gaining a foothold.

It is rare to see the content of our smear campaign originating in an e-mail or even a newspaper advertisement for instance from us. The key word here is originating. We prefer to start a smear campaign through word of mouth. E-mail and postings to social network sites may well follow at a later stage once the victim is aware of the smear campaign. This might be done by a lieutenant but there will be no link to us for reasons of plausible deniability and avoiding accountability for the act of spreading malicious lies or sensitive truths about a person.

Soon the smear campaign is taking a hold. It is hot gossip, interesting tittle tattle as it spreads through our supporters and then begins to wash onto the shores of your kingdom. It spreads since people love to share news, they enjoy gossiping and with the energy put behind it by my lieutenants and me, with no counter activity yet taking place it is in the best possible place to achieve traction.

Keeping the smear in an oral form enables it to spread quickly, be difficult to pin down so that when you do eventually find out you are chasing ghosts and allows us to deny what you have heard is accurate or is indeed anything to do with us. People love to talk and we want them to do so.

Once you as the victim knows about the smear campaign that is when there may well be a widening of it to take in more people through technology. Naturally if we posted the comments to social media sites at the outset you will be tipped-off far too quickly before the smear campaign has gained traction. However, it should have sufficient traction by the time you find out so that it no longer matters. This is when posting to forums, your social media sites, uploading videos and photographs will happen in order to inject additional energy into the smear campaign and also to cause you additional hurt and consternation. Those already infected by the smear will see this additional material as further evidence that they were right to believe us. Furthermore, people who had not been involved become infected and there is also the fact that many people, including those who may not even know you or me enjoy jumping in to a social media shit storm and flinging more mud around. The trolls will come out to play.

These postings will either be from us using false profiles or through lieutenants so that we can maintain plausible deniability in respect of any repercussions whilst extending the smear to a much wider audience through the use of technology.

The Types of Smear Campaign

The smear campaign is a regular weapon in our arsenal. Deployed, as I have explained, to maintain our façade and ensure that everybody thinks that you are the abuser, you are the trouble maker and that you are the Crazy One. They are used to discredit others, attack troublemakers and isolate them, have you bound closer to us and aid our seduction, dependent on who the smear campaign is aimed at. A method of getting our retaliation in first. The smear campaigns are such that the target will have no idea they are being carried out until the damage is done. You may find out through a third party tipping you off about what is being said about you. You may find out because we have instructed a lieutenant to tip you off once we are satisfied that the smear campaign has been embedded, in order to allow us to draw fuel from your horrified reaction and frantic attempts to repair the damage. Naturally, we only allow the tip off to take place once we are satisfied that our smears have sunk in and taken effect. The first you may know about these smear campaigns is when you try to tell other people about our behaviour, either during the relationship or when you have sought to escape or have been discarded. You find that you are met with shaking heads, blank looks and declarations of disbelief as your protestations are regarded with scepticism and whispered comments about you having lost the plot. To come up against this wall, especially when you are often in the greatest need, distressing. This distressing is magnified when it occurs with people you thought that you could rely on. Our poison seeps everywhere.

There are many different types of smear campaign that are used against you as a primary source, you as a defective appliance from the supplementary sources, you as an identified troublemaker, a stigmatised person and you as a predecessor primary source. Some are subtle, others are brutal and obvious and recognising them is key to tackling them. The methods used vary, the effects on you are as outlined above although they will vary in strength and intensity. Some will necessitate the use of complete lies, others will rely on the release of sensitive information and others take a grain of truth and distort it. There are hundreds of smear campaigns but I detail below a range of popular smear campaigns to aid your identification and understanding.

1. The Abuser

We like to trot out tales about how cruel and unpleasant you have been to us. Whether it is preventing us from seeing our friends, not letting us have our say, making decisions for us, hitting us, failing to attend to household chores whilst we are out working to support the household, not showing us any affection, questioning us about our movements, calling us names and so on, it will be used against you. Much of the smear campaign is based on projection as we tell everybody that you have been doing the very things that we have been doing. That way we can provide sufficient detail about the form of abuse, because we have done it ourselves, so that it is given the mantle of believability. If we furnish such detail and avoid vagueness, our lies are made all the more believable. All types of smear campaign operate on the basis of making you out to be abusive in some way. Some are specific, as you will see below, whereas this form of smear campaign is predicated on an avalanche of plausible behaviours which cover a vast spectrum of abusive actions towards us from locking us out of our own home at night because we went out with friends to tipping freezing cold water over us when sat in the bath and pretending it was a joke, from making us sleep on the floor to hiding our car keys when we needed to be somewhere. A long list of awful abuses will be detailed along with how much of a martyr we have been in trying to put up with them and make things better.

2. The Philanderer/The Slut

We play the card that we are not given any affection, love or sexual gratification by the abuser but more than that you are busy engaging in frequent affairs and one night stands with other people. We have given you chances after discovering what you have been doing, because we want to get things back on track. We have given you everything and this is how we are repaid. We are heart-broken by these repeated infidelities. We will identify people of the opposite sex that you are close to and pedal lies that "there is something going on" between you and them. Those people we know who enjoy some tittle tattle will be approached first in order to give the lies some "legs" so that they will not only believe what they have been told about you and the neighbour, you and your colleague and you and the gardener, but they will spread the smear even further. Add in some casual sexual encounters we have learned about, linked to the fact you work away/work in a bar/ are friendly and out-going then the lies gain more traction.

As with many smear campaigns it has two elements to it. The failure to behave in a good way towards us (which will allow us sympathy and understanding) and then disgust at your own behaviour which will result in people acting in a prejudiced way towards you. We gain fuel from the audience response to learning about the smear, we gain further fuel when we envisage or indeed see your response when you learn we have been telling everybody that you used to be a street hooker or that you have been engaged in a lesbian affair with a school teacher and we also cause the audience to visit their outraged reaction on you as well.

3. The Spender

We work hard each day to provide for you and all you do is sit around ordering things off the internet, going out to lunch, organising another home improvement and frittering away our hard-earned money. We make out that you are squandering the fruits of our labour by pointing to the recent purchase of some expensive shoes, conveniently leaving out that this is the first pair you have bought in two years and you saved up for them. The joint credit card which bears the hammering of our profligate spending will be attributed to you. Words such as fraud, leech and gold digger will be bandied around as we make you out to be a free loader who has taken considerable advantage of our hard-working nature and generosity.

4. The Lunatic

This smear campaign will involve heart-felt explanations to medical professionals about your behaviour in order to have them say that there could be something wrong but they would need to undertake a proper diagnosis. We will take from this informal consultation the part we want to hear and then spread this around to other people.

"Yes I was concerned about her behaviour and because I care, I mentioned it to Dr Whitecoat and he told me that it would appear that she has a mental health issue. I know, it is terrible but it explains so much of her erratic behaviour. The thing is, I don't know if she will allow herself to be treated. Of course she will insist that there is nothing wrong with her, but apparently that is what these people do, they have no insight that there is anything wrong with them."

Sound familiar at all? We will pick on entirely innocuous behaviours of yours and magnify them so they become regarded as problematic. Idiosyncrasies will be portrayed as aberrations from normal behaviour and of course the more you try to point out that is us and not you, the crazier you appear.

5. The Turncoat

In this smear campaign we actually place the focus of your horrible behaviour on not just us but other people as well. We spend our time telling other people the horrible things you have said about them behind their backs. Of course, since we are in a relationship with you, it stands to reason that what we are saying must be true, otherwise why would we make it up about the person we love. We maintain that we are telling the "victim" of your scurrilous comments so they can keep an eye out for it happening again and to be a little wiser in their engagements with you. This will be based on oral recollection, so difficult to prove, but often we will engage a lieutenant in corroborating our lies so that the recipient believes us and is too busy basking in their own indignant and annoyed reaction to test the veracity of what they are being told.

6. The Addict

You have a serious problem and the time has come to tell other people about it. You enjoy the occasional flutter on the horses. You actually have a huge gambling issue which incorporates the casino, slot machines, betting on line, frequent trips to the bookmakers and even betting on which of two rain drops will trickle down the pane the fastest. You may like a drink now and again and we will turn this into full blown alcoholism, showing off pictures of the empties in the over flowing recycling bin. Those empties are ours or are the product of a weekend party but we are not going to let that get in the way of our smear. You are addicted to sex, watching porn, trying to make us do things in the bedroom that we do not want to do, demanding sex on tap and demeaning us. Your recent weight gain, although nothing significant is used against you as evidence of addiction to food, the money you waste on take away food is really starting to stack up now and the salad section in the fridge only ever stocks cream cakes these days.

7. The Veiled Threat

This smear campaign works by relying on intimidation by the implicit suggestion that we are going to do something. We will put it about that we have some information about the victim which we are obliged to disclosure to the authorities which will land them in hot water. We do not say what it is however which provides us with several advantages.

- There is no suggestion we have said anything wrong;
- People will fill in the gaps for us by speculating as to what it actually is;
- The potential for denying it is huge, why we would we say we are going to do something? You know us, we would have just gone and done it wouldn't we?
- It sounds serious and therefore will catch people's attention
- When you learn about it you will be hampered in tackling it because you do not know precisely what it is. You will be trying to think of all the things you have done to ascertain if there is something we could base such a complaint on and this will not only increase your sense of anxiety but it will also increase your sense of being powerless. How can you stop something that you do not know what it is?

Intimidation is one of our manipulative tools and we will not shy away from using this device when it comes to smearing you. When we seduce you we do many thing and one of those things is the gathering of information about your weaknesses, your secrets, your fears and your vulnerabilities. We are adept at garnering information from you. This will be done under the auspices of helping you and apparently caring about you but it is nothing of the sort. This information is gathered for the purpose of stockpiling in our arsenal for later use against you. The intelligence we collect about your weaknesses will be used when we commence our devaluation of you. You will have given this information readily and now you find it is being used against you during the smear. The effect is devastating. Usually the dissemination of information about you, which exposes some secret, or weakness that you have will cause you considerable concern but moreover will have people gossiping readily about it.

This can range from something which you find embarrassing and that you would rather other people did not know through to those secrets which could cause you trouble with family, friends, your employment and possibly even the authorities. Rest assured that we would have such information about you because we make it one of our missions to obtain it from you during the seduction stage. We want to do this because: -

1.   It makes us look like we care about you so that you will bind yourself closer to us; and

2.   It provides us with ammunition to use during devaluation and also to form part of the Threats Power Play when we are attacking your implementation of No Contact (see **No Contact** for more)

You have no chance to avoid this scenario because you will always willingly give this information to us during the seduction because at that juncture you have no idea what you have been ensnared by. Accordingly, unless you have lived liked a saint and have no weaknesses whatsoever we will have gathered this required information about you.

We will threaten to act or release this information about you. We may also threaten to carry out certain acts against you. The more advanced of our kind will not make such threats in a form which has been documented to avoid the risk that you will then use this threat against us. There are two main ways in which this can happen. You will show it to other parties such as family and friends as evidence of what you have to put up with. This damages our façade and may turn popular opinion against us. Secondly, certain of our threats may stray into the criminal domain. Threats to damage your property, hurt you or others close to you. In such circumstances, the more advanced of our kind will be careful only to utter such threats against you in person when there are no witnesses and it is only you and I there. Our threats are effective for three reasons: -

1.   If they are based on your weaknesses then you know them to be true and you fear those weaknesses being exposed to a wider audience;

2   If they are based on your secrets you will again know them to be true and you will fear exposure; and

3.   If they are based on causing you harm (outside of the above two categories) you know from the behaviour exhibited during devaluation that it is no idle threat and that we are perfectly capable of taking such a step.

There is a high prospect of threats being used in a smear campaign against you because we will always have information available about you. Furthermore, if this smear is used against you as a Primary Source then your despicable act in going No Contact means that our ignited fury will erupt through the declaration of threats as we seek to lash out against you by using our fury as a weapon.

If you learn about the threatened action, you face a difficult decision. You cannot call our bluff. If you do not respond to our threat, then we will carry it out and therefore we will take a certain step and/or disseminate information about you to the authority. If we know something we will release it or we will make it up. At this point the smear campaign morphs in the smear campaign Criminal Activity (see below).

Alternatively, you take the dangerous step of trying to counter us and then you are at considerable risk of giving us fuel, upset further and also Hoovered. You are in an invidious position and we know this, this is why this type of smear campaign is especially good.

8. You Drove Us to the Point of Suicide

It is extremely rare for our kind to commit suicide. It does happen but it is very much the exception. The reason for this is that we have no desire to end our greatness and there is a school of thought which suggests you cannot kill someone who died in the emotional sense a long time ago. That however is a debate for another occasion. It tends to happen to those of our kind who have other co-morbid mental health issues. Ordinarily we are of the view that the world needs us and therefore why on earth would we remove ourselves from it? Of course this does not mean that we are above using the concept of suicide as a means by which to instigate a smear campaign. It will be used in conjunction with the Abuser smear campaign by detailing all of the horrible things that you have done to us but this time we go further. We let it be known that such was the level of your abuse that we tried to commit suicide. We tried to hang ourselves (but a loyal and witnessing lieutenant saved us). We took an overdose (but a loyal and witnessing lieutenant saved us). We were ready to jump off a bridge or building (but a loyal and witnessing lieutenant saved us. You get the picture

It is a powerful move on our part and is always destined to have the empathic individuals in the receiving audience come running so that we are able to engage with them. This act plays on the following: -

1.   The desire to prevent harm;

2.   The sense of guilt that you have caused us, the person you love, to end our life and our supporters feel this guilt in that they did not know what was going on and were not able to assist;

3.   The demonstration of our utter misery at being parted from you and thus the lashing of sympathetic fuel we shall receive from the audience.

We will fabricate evidence to show that this suicide was going to happen. A lieutenant will have messages to show to people, messages such as

"I can no longer live without x. Good bye."

"There is nothing to live for now I have lost x. Farewell."

"I am broken beyond repair by losing x and have no longer any need to live. I love x"

We will ensure that a lieutenant has a picture of us on the ledge, or they record the footage to show people. There will be a picture of scattered pills and an empty vodka bottle, the prepared noose. We will wear bandages on our otherwise unharmed wrists, all part of showing the extent to which we were pushed by you.

Heartless? Of course, but you know that is what we truly are.

In some instances, the lieutenant knows it is a concocted plan. In others, they actually believe we were going to kill ourselves. We will ensure we use a lieutenant in these machinations that will know exactly where to find us. The Lieutenant will present in a state of urgency and explain that he or she has just received a message along the lines of one of the above messages and will tell the audience which will add drama and weight to the smear campaign.

The Lieutenant will either find me feigning being distraught and sat there with a noose in my hands or the proverbial packet of pills and bottle of vodka nearby. We may even push it one step further for maximum effect and take a few of the pills and make ourselves appear woozy and out of it so the unwitting Lieutenant is particularly alarmed. There may even be a few half-hearted scratches at our wrists with a razor.

The Lieutenant, in the know or not, will readily disseminate the news of this terrible development that someone as wonderful as us has been pushed to the very brink by this awful person. We may not actually say what has caused us to be in this state. Other times we will refer to the abuse being such that we could not take any more or it is because this person has ended the relationship in such a cruel fashion after we gave our all. Whatever explanation is given this is a dramatic smear campaign which is particularly effective because people will be more concerned about out welfare and their disgust at how you caused this, than to be questioning whether it is true or not. Indeed, even if the audience has their suspicions as to the veracity of it all they know better than to face moral outrage by several people by speaking out.

9. **Sex**

If you have read my book **Sex and the Narcissist** you will be aware of just how powerful a tool sex is when wielded by us. It will come as no surprise to you that this remains the case when we are instigating a smear campaign. We are (save for the Victim Narcissist) accomplished in matters that take place between the sheets and this proves a highly addictive quality. Many victims of ours will often remark at how good the sex was, not all, but a lot do so. The sex we provide is based on extensive experience and delivered in a supercharged and heightened environment so that it is extremely memorable. This generates an addictive quality, which binds you to us quickly and tightly during the seduction. It also provides us with a means by which we can abuse our sexual brilliance to bring about highly effective devaluations. By the same token we will use the issue of sex to create a smear campaign about you. There is the philanderer/slut campaign as mentioned above but we also use sex in a different way as part of a smear campaign.

- To suggest that you have an overbearing voracious sexual appetite which meant you took liberties with us;
- You engage in bizarre and unpleasant fetishes;
- You engage in unlawful sexual practices;
- You withheld sex from us in order to punish us.

As with many smear campaigns we will often be projecting our own sexual preferences and behaviours as ones that you engage in. The sexual arena provides us with a huge choice ranging from the unusual, to the bizarre the sickening and the unlawful. Do not be surprised to find our internet browsing history being touted around as "yours" or for a phone containing certain memberships of fetish sights and pictures of an unsavoury nature be labelled as your phone which we have confiscated. It will not be your main phone of course. You still have that. We have purchased a 'phone and made it out to be yours. The emotional reaction and bias of the receiving audience will accept this content as clearly true as opposed to an objective and logical analysis of the situation. It is far more interesting to accept that you enjoy group sex with midgets than to question whether that it is true. Sex is always on interest to people and proves particular so as part of smear campaign.

I recall with particular fondness doing this with a former girlfriend Karen. She had a vast sexual appetite and therefore my proficiency in bed was something, which she found highly attractive during the seduction and thereafter, when I took it away from her, something that caused her grave consternation. She wanted sex often and regularly and she regarded it as the ultimate expression of love between two people. Karen placed great stock in the sexual act. I have to concede that she was very good in bed and was amenable to new ideas and techniques. She was not afraid to initiate them either although I always delighted in blocking such attempts so she understood who was in control. I was always able to bring her to heel by using sex. She craved it, demanded it and placed great value in the fact that we coupled in this way. She made a rod for her own back in this regard.

On the one occasion that Karen decided that she had had enough and sought to end matters with me, I deployed a smear campaign by suggesting that she like to engage in sex with strangers in hotel rooms. I used evidence of my own activity in that regard, credit card details etc., to support the suggestion. I also let it be known that she had a particular fetish which involved multiple strangers ejaculating over her. People knew she was a sensual and sexual person and therefore this fallacy was not too great a jump for them to make. This sexual practice coupled with her repeated infidelity formed a delicious and salacious smear campaign which soon gained traction. People spread this information around with ease and I know that it permeated where she worked which caused her additional difficulties. Hers was an instance where the sordid nature of her nocturnal activities meant that she found such fabricated exposure especially hurtful. I then applied a Sexual Power Play as part of the hoover (see **No Contact** for more) and the tenderising effect of the smear campaign and the Power Play meant she was putty in my hands. Again.

10.Destruction

I have in the past used a destructive tendency as part of the control of victims. The smashing up of property and a property has a particular method of causing someone to be more focussed. I have used this method as part of a hoover but then have used the photographs of the destruction in order to smear somebody who is known as having a temper to portray that person as destructive and nasty.

I once shared a home with Alex. You may recall that she was gymnast. I owned the property but she lived there with me, having sold her own house and deposited the funds in her bank account for an as yet undefined later use. It was a Thursday and when I returned from work I found that she was not there but a note was left in clear view on the occasional table in the living room.

"Dear HG, I have had enough. I do still love you but I cannot live with you. I have moved out. Please do not contact me until I have had time to recover. I will make arrangements to collect the rest of my possessions. Alex xxx"

I crumpled the note up in the palm of my hand as the fury rose inside of me. How dare she? How dare she walk out like this after all the things that I had done for her. The flames of my anger grew and rose, surging up inside as I found myself twisting left and right looking for a way to vent my rage. A torrent of abuse spilled from my lips as I became consumed by my anger. This woman had insulted me with her departure. She had not even had the decency to tell me to my face, after all the support I had given her, letting her live with me and shuttling to and from her gymnastic competitions. The ungrateful bitch. My sense of injustice was huge and with the firmest of reasons for feeling that way.

I marched over to the sideboard where her numerous trophies were displayed and picked up the largest. I twisted and pulled at the plastic until it snapped and then grabbed the next one. I bent it and then hurled it to the floor. A third trophy was selected and I dented the metal with my fists as I pounded it. I worked my way through all of her trophies, snapping, breaking and pummelling as my animated self was reflected in the mirror on the wall. Had I stopped to look at myself I would have seen the mask of hatred that was pulled tight across my face. I made my way into the garden. It was a summer evening and I made a fire in the brazier at the end of the garden before returning to the living room. I snatched up two of the largest trophies, now mangled and misshapen and hurled them into the flames and watched as the plastic began to melt, the metal started to blacken and the wood caught fire.

I returned to the house and made for the bookcase. I hauled all the books that belonged to her from the bookcase and took them to the brazier. I tore each book down its spine as I imagined I was tearing Alex in two, before dropping the rent apart novel into the orange flames. Two pictures that she loved were next. I took a knife to them slashing them and then hanging them back up. She could look on them when she tried to recover them. I surged up the stairs and into our bedroom. I flung open the wardrobe and found many of her clothes had already been moved, but still some remained. Like a dervish, I assaulted the suits and dresses, slashing at them with the knife in my hand, as if I was stabbing and slashing Alex. The garments, now shredded and in ribbons hung from the rail or slipped forlornly to the floor. I scooped up some shoes and took them outside and added them to the flames. Back in the bedroom I opened the drawers on the nightstand and rifled through to find she had not taken her passport. I shoved that into my suit pocket. I decided I would keep that to use as leverage.

I made my way to the bathroom and found that most of her toiletries had been removed, but of those left they were emptied into the sink, their contents squeezed from them and the perfume bottles smashed on the tiled floor leaving an overpowering cloud of scent as the contents leaked across the tiles. I stormed into the study and noticed she had taken her laptop and her tablet but she had not touched the PC, which belonged to me. I switched it on and as I broke another picture she liked over my knee I began to delete the pictures she had stored on the PC. I entered the kitchen and grabbed the scales she used to measure out her food as part of her fitness regime. I found a hammer from under the sink and smashed and dented the scales with the hammer. Opening a cupboard, I saw her favourite mug and that was hurled to the floor so it shattered on the ground. My eye fell on the champagne flutes that she liked. We had bought them together but she liked them so one by one I cast them onto the ground as the glass fractured and broke. Next was a set of plates she had picked. I bought them but they could go next, the crockery smashing and spilling across the floor as I slammed them downwards. I could always buy more plates.

Still my anger raged as I prowled back and forth through the house looking for anything that she owned or liked which I could consign to the inferno outside or smash under the hammer that I wielded. Perhaps an hour later I sat at the base of the stairs, my chest rising and falling from the exertion, the product of my destruction lying all around, the smell of smoke drifting in from the garden. I pulled out my phone and began to record all of the carnage, the ripped clothes, the shattered utensils, the battered trophies and the still burning books before I sent the video to her number and then I was finally able to smile as the surge of power took over from the burning rage. At the same time, I sent this to two of my lieutenants and called them telling them that I had just walked in to find that Alex had smashed up the house. I wanted people to believe that my destruction was hers and instructed my lieutenants to start spreading the news of her orgy of destruction. I reasoned that if the video footage sent to Alex was sufficient to have her return so I could apply a hoover, I would just blame the lieutenants for sending the footage elsewhere. If she returned but the hoover was unsuccessful she would at least be preoccupied with me as the destructive smear campaign footage began to do the rounds and then I could follow this up with choice telephone calls to those that mattered, pointing out how wildly she had behaved. She had not only smashed up our things but she was that unhinged that she had smashed up her own belongings and possessions. The video footage could not be argued with. It did not show me smashing things up but rather the aftermath of someone having done it. Of course Alex would deny it but then she would wouldn't she, smashing up the home like this and she was known for being fiery. I, by contrast, through the façade I had created was the very model of calm and reason. If the smear campaign had to be relied on, then I would be able to do so with considerable conviction.

Alex also made the error of leaving in her nightstand drawer her emergency credit card. I knew that she did not carry it with her to avoid the temptation to spend on it. Instead, she kept it hidden away to use should there be some emergency. It was evident that she had forgotten it. I took the opportunity to go on a spending spree. I ordered some sex toys in her name and sent them to her work and her parent's address. I sent pizzas to all the neighbours. I booked a break for me in a fortnight's time. I also ordered a succession of self-help books and analysis books dealing with Borderline Personality Disorder and sent them to her sister's address. That made me laugh as I thought how that would certainly kick the hornet's nest between the two of them. I also: -

1. Bought jewellery for two prospects I was pursuing;
2. Replaced the crockery that I had smashed up;
3. Bought tickets to various shows which I then gave away to my junior colleagues receiving a delicious burst of admirable fuel in the process;
4. Organised a funeral wreath bearing her name to be sent to her parents' house;
5. Purchased a painting I had wanted as a little reward for my inventive and hard work.

The upshot of her leaving such an item in my possession was that she incurred a rather large shock when the credit card bill arrived which followed on from the various fallouts that arose from the transactions that I had engaged in. This also allowed me to use this spending spree as a legitimate response to her behaviour. I had to replace everything that she had broken and it was only right that I used her credit card and compensated myself for the inconvenience. Not only was I able commence a smear campaign as an insurance policy, I was able to then engage in further behaviour which would rile her and cause her to give me fuel, under the auspices of compensation and reparation.

8.10 The White Knight

This smear campaign plays on the idea that I am a white knight who rode to the victim's rescue and I gave them everything and how did they repay me? They walked out. I may use this as a stand-alone as described above or in conjunction with a smear campaign suggesting that the victim is an abuser.

This smear campaign focusses more on what I have done, all the good behaviour, the generosity and the kindness that I have exhibited. I utilise the façade to considerable effect and against this backdrop of decency I point out how terrible this person has been by contrast. Either the act of walking away from someone so noble as me is bad enough but then if I add the abuser scenario as well that victim is made to look even worse.

If you have left us, as a consequence of our abuse, we recognise that you will be upset and distressed by what has happened, by feeling the need to leave us and no doubt putting yourself in a difficult position across a number of fronts. You may be in temporary accommodation, you may face financial difficulties, be away from your family and friends. We will have this worked out already and indeed we will have engineered some if not all of these difficulties that you now find yourself in as a consequence of firstly your involvement with me and secondly (and this is what we will focus on) your desire to escape me.

When we first seduced you, we looked to be the white knight that comes riding to your rescue. Invariably, because of the conditioning that society subjects people to and in particular women, there still remains the concept of the damsel in distress being liberated by the knight in shining armour. Of course this is an insult to all the independent, secure and self-sufficient women who are successful and fulfilled in many aspects of their lives. I however need not be troubled with whether they feel insulted or offend by this indoctrination because there remains a significant part of the female population that subscribes either consciously or sub-consciously to this ideal. Consequently, the concept of the arrival of the white knight on his charger is a concept, which lends itself to my seduction of you. Having used this as part of my campaign of love-bombing once and thus imbued inside of you the image of how I am here to help and rescue you, allied with my knowledge that you want to be rescued and protected, I know that deploying such a technique when I am smearing you, is likely to meet with success.

Not only will I smear you by showing how ungrateful you have been, I will continue to demonstrate how decent I am by the fact that I will come riding to the rescue, resplendent on my horse, armour shining and lance tilted ready to slay the dragon which plagues you (no not ourselves!). This will manifest through

- Depositing money in your bank account
- Arranging accommodation for you, say at a hotel or a rented property
- Organising child minding
- Arranging transport for you
- Attending to administrative matters on your behalf

- Catering for medical issues

Choose any issue which may be causing you some consternation and at the outset of the smear campaign we will suddenly appear having addressed the issue on your behalf. This step is taken in order to tap into the sense of natural gratitude you should exhibit at having had a difficult situation resolved or made less onerous. The audience will expect you to express your thanks because you have been brought up to do so and behave politely and because yet again, even when provoked by your horrible behaviour, we have done the right thing, something good. People will be aghast at your behaviour following how well we have behaved and not only that they will be more inclined to support us as a consequence of seeing how selflessly we act and how noble we are in the face of your provocative behaviour. We truly are a white knight. We garner fuel from appreciate and admiring audience members whilst their distaste for your lack of gratitude continues thus smearing you further.

12 False Criminal Allegations

We threaten to proceed with a criminal complaint against you either based on fact or more likely something invented. It does not matter that there is only our word to support it, this will at least result in an investigation and your likely arrest. This will cause you anxiety and upset and we will embellish the details, rope in a Lieutenant to support our false complaint and ensure that you have the prospect of humiliation at best and incarceration at worst hanging over you. The Greater Narcissist usually takes this step as it is a particular malicious step to take which has no regard at all for the truth of the matter, nor the actual consequences which may arise for us by making a false complaint. Of course we do not care about those consequences because they will not apply to us. We will be able to talk our way out of them as we can with everything.

The intention of this smear campaign is to use the criminal agencies to locate you and obtain that information for our use. It is then to put you under pressure and generate anxiety for you. The prospect of a criminal conviction may have ramifications for you concerning your employment (thus we attack another support network in this manner), it will support our discrediting of you by convincing your supporters that you are the trouble maker and it will seek to cause them to switch their allegiance to me instead.

You will feel angered by this injustice but the seriousness of it will hammer your reputation considerably, generate repercussions and have many people judging you. The concept of innocent until proven guilty goes out of the window with gossip. You are guilty the moment you are seen being arrested by the police, watched by neighbours.

. Naturally we will be content to drop the complaint and explain how it was all a mistake or how we have reconciled our differences and no longer wish to proceed with the case if we later wish to hoover you. We will not do this however until we know we have pulled you back in to our sphere of influence.

We will deploy this smear campaign to cause you considerable distress and anxiety. Even if you confront us and provide us with fuel, begging us to stop the process we will use this as evidence of your guilt and escalate matters by suggesting you are now threatening us in order to stop the investigation.

How might you deal with this? You have no option other than to defend yourself and fight it. This means that the audience will regard the content of the smear campaign as being accurate because the investigation is ongoing. They can see you are worried by it; therefore, it must be true.

It will be difficult for you to tackle this smear campaign, as you may find yourself facing a serious accusation and with our accomplices supporting our version of event your prospects may seem slim. However, you will be forced to fight the complaint. It is unlikely that we will back down and you will have to hope that the prosecuting authority decides against proceeding with it or you are acquitted at trial, unless the smear campaign is then used to soften you up for a hoover. If you agree to return, we will drop the charges and this smear campaign as worked both as a smear campaign and as a way to get you to come back to us through a hoover at a later stage.

There will be all manner of inventive and scurrilous accusations. Allegations that you have assaulted us and/or stolen from us are the most common and you can expect these to be regularly used in respect of a smear campaign. Allegations of sexual crimes, fraud at work, fiddling expenses, drink driving and shoplifting are also common. Do not put it past us to set you up for some of these crimes by notifying the police when we know you have drunk too much to be driving or by having someone steal from a shop and place it in your house. We will of course have gathered a lot of information about you and any petty misdemeanours you might have committed at some point will be used against you as well. As ever with the smear campaign we will look to use a grain of truth or invent it but ensure it has the air of being plausible. Criminal proceedings carrying significant stigma and may also be spread by the media. This creates a significant Majority Effect whilst causing further harm to you.

13 The Poor Parent

This smear campaign is used by our kind to demonstrate that the victim is a poor parent. The campaign is not so much suggesting that there is out and out abuse of the children (although this may well be a form of the campaign which manifests) but rather that the parenting skills of the victim are below par. If there is a suggestion of actual abuse this may have some unwelcome comeback for our kind in terms of our involvement or a failure to protect the children. Whilst we are content to use law enforcement agencies in terms of criminal allegations as described above, we do not want to lose control of the campaign and nor do we want unwelcome attention placed on ourselves. With those considerations in mind, this type of smear campaign will focus on the ineptitude of the other parent in terms of incompetence and a lack of consideration for the children by alleging such things as: -

- Failure to provide meals that are sufficiently nutritious
- Not washing the children often enough
- Not washing the clothes of the children often enough
- Failing to change bedding;
- Being asleep when the children need attention;
- Not playing with the children;
- Failing to assist with homework
- Not turning up for school activities (presentations and sports days for example)
- Swearing in front of the children or even at them;

- Being drunk in front of the children;
- Failure to chastise the children or excessive chastisement

These examples will be used in a cumulative fashion as well. We will often use this tactic when we are working and the victim is at home, therefore we have an automatic defence when someone asks us what we have done about it. We can declare,

"I do as much as I can but I am at work. Someone has to pay the bills."

Attacking someone's parenting skills is effective because everybody has differing standards when it comes to raising children. For example, if you take the issue of discipline, people have varying attitudes to how this should be done. This means that you may not have done something wrong but we can portray it in a different light to people who perhaps may be firmer disciplinarians and thus they take a dim view of the light touch the victim applies in this area.

The attack against the victim's parenting skills is a particularly emotional smear campaign. By expressing our concern, we are see once again as the kind and considerate party. The audience will want to do the right thing, after all, children are at stake here. This is especially effective in terms of affecting the attitudes of the victim's family and friends. It also means that when the victim finds out about this then he or she will react in a greater emotional fashion and provide us with fuel.

14. The Liar

Another substantial piece of projection by us as we propound our own lies each and every day but twist matters around to create a smear campaign where you are castigated as the liar. We will throw the whole book of lies at you – white lies, dangerous lies, lies about us, lies about other people, huge lies, lies that are based on exaggeration, lies which are designed to hurt other people, lies about lies. The stance that is adopted is to suggest that you are a pathological liar and that you lie with consummate ease so that you no longer know what the truth is and what a lie is. We will use our skills at twisting conversations by expressing, with our considerable powers of conviction that you are a habitual liar. What we will do is recount conversations between you and I but we will reverse the roles so that where we have told lies we will make it seem as if you have. This is a device that is applicable to the Greater of our kind. The Lesser Narcissist will just make up the lies, since he or she will not possess the high enough function to recall the conversations in sufficient detail.

Expect to find out that comments such as these will have been used in the smear campaign against you: -

"She just cannot stop telling lies."

"She said that you (meaning the audience member) said that about me. I didn't believe it of course but that is the kind of thing that she says about people."

"He has no friends because of his lies."

"I am concerned his lies will get him into trouble at work."

"Everything is an exaggeration. He has such and such a car, he has been to so many places, he is going to buy a larger house and so on. He cannot help it. If someone says they have a jet ski, he has two. It is ridiculous."

"I am so tired of being lied to. It is gone beyond a joke now, there is something seriously wrong with him."

"I have caught her lying on so many occasions I have lost count. It doesn't matter if they are big or small, she has told lies. She lies saying she hasn't eaten something when it is clearly her. She lies about where she has been, even though I have seen her at a bar."

"I am concerned that the lying won't stop and she will get herself into some serious trouble."

This smear campaign is particularly about managing expectations. By causing people to believe that you tell a lot of lies, when you confront the audience about the smear campaign and deny it, they are bound to think that this is just more lying on your part. You react and they automatically fall foul of thinking "she protests too much so it must be true". The smear campaign is effective and damaging. The fact is that everybody tells lies at some point so there will be plenty of material to work with and also with a supporting cast from the lieutenants and coterie we are able to call on willing witnesses to testify to your mendacious nature.

15. Fake Concern

We will use this in conjunction with another smear campaign for example addiction whereby not only will we fabricate that you have a problem with drink, we will then express false concern about how it is affecting you and other people. Our ability to fabricate concern is well known and we are able to portray a concerned partner with the appropriate expressions, statements and inflections of tone. We will talk about how: -

"I am concerned for his health."

"She is drinking herself to death at this rate."

"I have noticed money is going missing to fund this gambling habit."

"I have tried talking to him but I cannot get him to listen. That is why I am turning to you in the hope that you can say something that will make him take notice."

"I am at my wit's end with it all. It just keeps getting worse. I need your help to get her some help."

Nobody is going to turn down someone who has such kind-hearted and compassionate motives. By layering the content of the smear campaign with this faked concern we maximise its effectiveness. It can also be used as a stand-alone smear campaign as well: -

"I don't what it is but he has been acting strangely as of late."

"I can't work it out but there is something definitely wrong."

"I don't know what is behind it, but her behaviour has gone from bad to worse and I need to get her some help."

"I am troubled by her behaviour. Is there anything you know about her when she was younger which might help me?"

If you resist this offer of help from me and others, the audience will conclude that you are in denial. If you accept the help, then you have conceded that there is something wrong and we have succeeded in having the smear ratified and verified by you. You are damned if you do and damned if you don't.

16. Socially Unacceptable Behaviours

These behaviours may not be unlawful in the context of holding certain opinions but in right-thinking society they are certainly regarded with concern and disapproval. We will seize on some remark you may have made to label you as belonging to a particular prejudicial group or be of a bigoted nature and then use that as the basis of the smear campaign to tell people that you have learned of this prejudice and you find it distasteful. That is why the relationship has ended. You will warn people about this and of course this smear campaign is particularly effective if the audience group contains members who would be affected by this fabricated prejudice on the part of the victim.

We will endeavour to paint you as: -

- Racist
- Homophobic
- Sexist
- Holding unsavoury views about children
- A sexual deviant
- Scathing about people with disabilities

In order to ensure that you are met with disapproval from the audience group.

17. Drama Queen

The victim is painted as being melodramatic and always causing a scene. This smear campaign is often used when stigmatising an individual over time. The fundamentals of this smear campaign are as follows: -

- Diminishing your credibility because whilst you may not lie, you make a drama out of anything and everything;
- Questioning your perspective of events because you over-react;
- Demonstrating that you are a wearing person to be around because of this heightened state (whereas of course if you are a drama queen we love it because of all the fuel we receive)
- That you cannot be trusted to over-react to a situation thus making it worse
- That you cannot be trusted to spoil things because you make it all about yourself because of your propensity to be dramatic.

Once again this is a classic piece of projection on our part. Expect to hear comments about you such as: -

"Getting dressed in the morning is turned into a circus."

"Nothing is straightforward with her."

"We cannot sit and enjoy a meal in peace without there being some histrionics."

"Every birthday has been spoilt by his need to make a scene."

"I am losing friends because of this behaviour. We don't get invited to as many dinner parties as we once did because of the way she goes on."

18. The User

This smear campaign paints you as someone who is only ever in it for yourself. Your friends are just methods of achieving things for your own benefit. You only contact family when you want something and everybody is expendable. Sound like anybody you know? Certainly not you but we will make it seem like it is you by propounding tales based on how you have said things behind people's backs, that you are only friends with someone because of their wealth, that you are only bothering with a parent in order to secure an inheritance and so forth. You do not care about anybody and only ever do something if there is some favourable outcome for you involved in it. People are expendable, they are to be drained and utilised for your advantage. You borrow items and never return them. Borrow money and do not repay it. You expect people to do things for you without reward or thanks. We especially like to explain how not only do you behave like this towards us but you also do take advantage of the people in the audience group.

19. Incompetent

This is often used to stigmatise an individual as part of a long running and slow burning smear campaign. The put downs are scathing about an individual's competence. This competence will cover various areas including: -

- Education
- Parenting
- Social skills
- Sporting ability
- Emotional intelligence
- DIY work
- Career
- Domestic chores

You can expect to hear comments along the lines of: -

"Every time he produces a hammer I know something will get broken."

"I know he tries god love him but he is useful."

"He will never amount to anything. He is useless."

"I have never known anybody but him unable to use a washing machine."

"I wouldn't say her cooking was terrible but even the dog won't touch her meals."

"There are no straight shelves in our house. He thinks he is great with tools but he is hopeless."

"He will be lucky if he passes one subject."

"She won't get anywhere at work. She is a worker bee. Nothing special."

By repeatedly stating these things we will create a complete lack of expectation concerning the victim. It also allows highlighting to be achieved. This is where we highlight a fault or failing so that the victim is known for it and therefore every time they do something wrong it is regarded as par the course for this individual regardless of whether in actual fact they commit few mistakes and other people may actually make more but this has not been highlighted and therefore is not picked up on.

20. The Contrarian

Again this is often used for the purposes of stigmatising an individual. This is where the victim is made out to argumentative, awkward and adopting a contrary stance to whatever is said, irrespective of whether the victim actually believes that stance or not. They are a devil's advocate and a royal pain in the backside. Of course, once again this is projection on our part. You can expect us to make comments such as: -

"He can start an argument in an empty room."

"Whatever I say he always takes the opposite stance."

"Whatever I suggest she takes issue with."

"He just likes to argue for the sake of it."

"She can never admit she is wrong."

"He never says sorry because he thinks his position is always right."

"If I say the sun is shining, he would say it is raining just so he can take a different stance to me."

"He always has to find some fault, something that is wrong in order to be awkward."

"There is always some reason for him to complain."

You are portrayed as miserable, argumentative and a serial complainer. You are made out as difficult to live with, a person who is a damp squib on otherwise enjoyable occasions and someone who revels in making life difficult for everyone around them by persisting with such an attitude. You are a curmudgeon, a kill joy and a professional miserabilist.

21. Jealousy

This smear campaign operates on the basis that you are jealous of me (and possibly other people, those in the smear audience and thus the smear campaign acquires greater effectiveness). The jealousy might be because of the friendship we have with somebody in the smear audience, the fact we are successful, sporty, artistic, interesting, good at our job, sociable and so on. We will select one or more of our positive character traits and then explain how the victim is jealous of that trait and this has caused considerable traits. You can expect comments such as: -

"I cannot help the fact that people like me, but she turns into the green-eyed monster whenever I talk to other women."

"I cannot talk about my job to him you know. It seems to wind him up because my job is of a higher status than his. I have worked hard for both of us and I just wish he could be pleased for me instead of being envious."

"I keep fit and look after myself but she just accuses me of being vain and self-obsessed. It is plain jealousy and not very pleasant."

"No matter what I do it is always shot down. It is as if I am not allowed to do anything good because it reminds her of her own failings."

Countering the Smear Campaign

So, we now turn to what you can do about the smear campaign. The significant advantage I can convey to you is to detail how we respond to certain actions and what we may do in response so that you are given the information about how the person you are dealing with is likely to behave. This is unrivalled knowledge.

This is divided into two sections; before it begins and once you know about it.

1. Before It Begins

You may not think it but you do actually have the ability to exert control over the smear campaign before it actually begins. There are two occasions where this arises. One situation does afford you more power than the other. The first occasion is where you make the decision.

a. You Make the Decision

If you have decided that you will end the relationship and you will do so on your terms and at a time of your choosing, you can have a massive impact on nullifying the smear campaign that we will try to use against you. What is the overriding reason why our smear campaigns succeed? There are many factors behind its success as I have detailed above but the overriding reason is because **we get in**

first. When you make the decision you are able to get in first. In order to succeed in life there are generally three things one must do. Be the best, cheat or be first. Being the best with our kind will not help you as this is likely to mean you are the best at providing fuel. You cannot cheat when it comes to a smear campaign, but you can be first.

I recommend you have regard to **Departure Imminent: Preparing For No Contact to Beat the Narcissist** as these contains a wealth of information to assist you in the preparatory stage to ensure that your no contact works and also avoids being derailed before it begins. The information about identifying and utilising a small group of loyal supporters is of considerable importance.

If you get in first, you will achieve the following benefits with regard to the forthcoming smear campaign: -

- You will have a group of supporters who will ring fence you and help you during a difficult time;
- You will have more energy available to deal with the smear campaign;
- Your supporters will be nearly unassailable in terms of us trying to infect them;
- You stand a better chance of "waverers" coming out on your side because you supporters will provide your own Majority Effect so that these undecided people will either withdraw and not help either side or assist you because they see that other people are. You may even gain critical mass through this method so that more

people accept your version and therefore this sways more and more people so that the smear campaign grinds to a halt;

- You present in a calm and reasoned manner when explaining why you are leaving us, most likely able to provide evidence and there is more time available for that person to process what you are telling them so they make up their own mind. The fact that a potential audience member is able to make up his or her mind is instrumental in ensuring that person accepts your evidence but also is not persuaded to the contrary;

- You can present information in a manner to head off the smear campaign rather than reacting to it. It is always easier to win a battle from a position of strength rather than where you are constantly reacting to the shifting ground and tactics of your opponent. You need to be on the front foot and not the back foot.

- As I shall explain, one of the most important things about the smear campaign is not to engage in the smear campaign. If you can organise your supporters first, appraise them of the facts, make all other preparations and then raise the drawbridge when the waves of the smear campaign come crashing towards you and others you are sat dry and elevated away from the carnage and therefore have no need to embrace it. You have made your point, you have your supporters and you need not consider the smear campaign at all. With your supporters (not you) countering it on your behalf, the tide may be turned so that it never gains traction and indeed blows up in our faces. Alternatively, it may burn out quicker without having any real effect.

Accordingly, there are considerable benefits to your pre-emptive strike.

What should you do in terms of getting in first?

- Organise and prepare for your departure
- Identify those people who you consider as instrumental in assisting you implement no contact and escape us and who will not be turncoats who will alert us as to what you are doing. This requires careful work.
- Once identified explain to those people what you are doing and why. Avoid instigating your own smear campaign as this will be counter-productive. Do not say
- "I am leaving him because he is an evil bastard who treats me like crap. I have put up with him playing around, being a drunkard and a useless dad. He never helps me around the house, the slob, he is crafty though, he always makes out that it is my fault and that I am somehow crazy, for instance (and then launch into a tirade of emotional examples) "

Whilst it may be tempting and indeed cathartic to list the whole litany of our abuses towards you, you are playing into our hands. The more you say the more potential there is for us to poke holes in what you have said. This will then diminish your credibility. Also you may be talking to people who know us as well and therefore they will not want to hear us being lambasted in such a way.

Furthermore, if you list a huge range of poor behaviours then this clashes with the façade and will cause people to begin to doubt what you are saying. You might think that the longer the list the more likely people will be to believe what you are saying but that is not the case. You would be far better served stating,

"I am leaving x. I have made this decision after careful consideration. It is not necessary for me to go into detail other than to tell you, as a trusted friend, that I have been badly treated and I am unable to tolerate it any longer. I have tried to resolve matters with x, but that has not worked. I must do this for my own peace of mind (and that of the children etc.) and I hope I can rely on your support in what will be a difficult period of time. I know x may contact you and he is likely to tell lies about me. I will happily address any of those concerns if you wish to raise them with me but I do not wish to dignify those lies by going into detail now, I am sure you will understand that."

This places the emphasis on you, helping you and behaving in an appropriate manner. This will increase the likelihood of you being helped by people. Once you have secured their assistance you may choose to provide some detail if you deem it necessary to deal with questions but confine it to things which have happened (rather than perceptions of behaviour i.e. I know it seems like he is being nice but he is actually putting me down in his way – that creates doubt and will only serve to make you look paranoid and crazy, things we try to paint you as). Do not rant or wail about the behaviour but explain it as calmly as you can.

If you know there are specific things that we are likely to say, for instance veiled threats about them have been made during devaluation, you can again get in first by explaining to your supporters what is likely to happen and provide your calm, fact-based version first so that it embeds in the mind of your supporters. You do not need to create a coven which is intent on slaughtering us with lengthy wine-fuelled sessions about what utter bastards we are. This will be seized on by us as showing how histrionic and unbalanced you are when the smear begins. If you provide us with an advantage, no matter how slight, we will seek to exploit it.

You will be in a position to remove those social media sites or block our access to those sites which we may use to post the material that is part of the smear campaign to.

You can organise legal representation and have this prepared in advance of our actions, rather than playing catch-up.

Do not attempt to persuade anybody who is in our camp (even if the suspicion is slight) as you will fail in your attempt and you run a huge risk of tipping us off about your imminent departure which will unravel all of your work so far.

When you decide to end the relationship you are able to put in place measures so that when the smear campaign does inevitably occur you neutralise many of its effects because you got in first. You may even be so effective as to neutralise it as whole because more people accept what you are your supporters say because you made the first move. Accordingly, when you are planning your escape you should also factor in how to deal with the smear campaign which will be unleashed against you.

b. Knowing It is About To Happen

For whatever reason you may not have planned an escape or it is still in progress when you realise that the smear campaign is about to happen against you. You will not have as much time to counter it in the way that is described above but knowing that it is coming will allow you to take some of the steps described above in order to protect yourself from the effects of the smear campaign.

How do you know that it is about to happen? You should look out for the following: -

- A charm offensive on our part to recruit more supporters. This is the single largest give away of what is about to happen as we seek to bolster our ranks for the smear campaign;
- Repeated mentions of somebody else. This is the new prospect and the more we talk about them (in order to triangulate you and gain fuel) the closer you are to being discarded and the smear campaign (you are being smeared to the new prospect already as a

predecessor but it will get worse and wider once you have been discarded).

- Repeated absences which are unexplained. We are organising the discard, marshalling the new prospect and readying to unleash the smear campaign by disappearing to our operational bolthole;

- Unusual responses from people. If you notice a "cooling" of behaviour from certain people, they have been primed for the smear campaign. They will not have been told what it is but may have been told to keep their distance from you.

Look out for these indicators as there is a very good chance that you are not far from the coming smear campaign. You should act to marshal your own supporters above everything else and do so as a matter of priority. If you achieve this and there has been no discard then attend to other matters as detailed above, but do not delay, the discard and smear is coming.

2. During the Smear Campaign

You may not have been able to organise a pre-emptive strike or even sense the coming smear campaign and the first you know is when people are no longer bothering with you and then news reaches your ears that the rumour is you have been having multiple affairs behind our backs. What should you do now that the smear campaign is up and running? There are actually many things you can do and also many things you should NOT do which are of equal validity in assisting you from getting through the smear campaign. Before I address those it is worthwhile you understanding what we picture you doing so you know how we are thinking.

When you first hear about the nature of the smear campaign we picture you astonished, angry, upset and ranting against it. You will be raw with emotion, disbelieving that we could do this and therefore this will provide us with considerable fuel. You will be amazed at the projection that is involved, how we are able to accuse you of the very things we do. You will have a massive sense of injustice, you will want to strike out, correct the smear, set the record straight and confront us. You will want to know why we are doing this. You will want to tell people that the smear is wrong and you will want them all to know how despicable we are. You will be frustrated, annoyed and beside yourself as this further blow against you. Your need to tackle the smear will be overwhelming and you will be governed by your emotions meaning that you will make numerous errors which will only heighten your distress, support the smear and play into our hands.

When you are aware that you are the victim of a smear campaign, you should have regard to the following: -

a. Remove emotion. As you know, your emotional reactions provide us with fuel. This is what we want and need. We want to picture your emotive response and then we want to see it as you confront us, challenge audience members and behave in an emotional fashion. Do not fall into this trap. Allow yourself an emotional outburst in private or with a trusted supporter and then do your best to turn off the tap. All actions thereafter must be conducted without emotion. You need to be business-like, as if reading the news. The removal of emotion is paramount because: -

This is what we want – fuel;

You will make poor decisions whilst in a heightened emotional state; and

You will lose supporters

b. Do not try and make us accountable for the smear (save legal action see below) because we do not do accountable, you will fail and most likely react in an emotional manner and thus provide us with fuel.

c. Do not fight fire with fire. You will fail. If you decide to come out all guns blazing and being nasty about us, you will only do the following: -

Give us fuel;

Lose credibility in front of supporters;

Galvanise our supporters;

Support the content of the smear ("told you she was horrible")

d. Do not try to smear us. This will fail. Do not try to spread rumours about us as we see this as desperation on your part, it gives us fuel and also allows us to reinforce what we have said about you.

e. Do not think that others can persuade us. You may be tempted to try to ask people to "have a word" with us in order to stop the smear campaign. This will fail because: -

The people may not want to get involved;

They may well be our supporters and they will refuse whilst telling us what you are doing;

We will utilise this as evidence of what a manipulative person you are to underline the nature of the smear.

f. Do not confront us. We want this We thrive on confrontation and we cannot wait for you to appear with a tear-stained face to beg, cajole and plead with us to leave you alone. We hope for this to happen above all else because it makes us feel powerful and gives us huge amounts of fuel. If you fail to confront us this will infuriate us. You may really want to call us all the names under the sun, point out our hypocrisy and so forth but all you will do is give us fuel and the smear will not stop. You are far better served by not responding to it by not responding to us. Believe me, we will hate that. You won't be able to see it but you can envisage our infuriated frustration at your failure to engage.

g. Use the threat of legal action if the smear will affect your livelihood in some way. Whilst we will deny and try to frustrate the action, it is likely to cause the lesser of our kind to back down. The greater will engage in order to try to succeed in the legal battle but eventually we will be forced to retreat. You in the meanwhile have sent out a powerful signal which will be noticed by the audience members. This means they will not want to be drawn into the legal fight and therefore whilst you won't stop us immediately, you will take a lot of energy out of the smear by causing many people to stop repeating it. Save legal action for threats to your livelihood rather than just being because you don't like what is being said. This is because you gain more credibility for taking such a step to preserve your livelihood and audience members will engage with and understand this to a greater degree.

If you say,

"He has been calling me a whore to everyone I know, I am going to slap a defamation case on him." People will think you should just turn the other cheek, not be so concerned about name-calling and possibly regard it as such an over-reaction it must be true!

Instead if you say,

"He gave me no choice but to instruct a lawyer. His comments to my employer threatened my livelihood and that of my children,"

or

"He has told lies to my licensing authority and that will affect my prospects of earning an income."

People will be far more understanding.

Engage a lawyer who is experienced in defamation and also ensure that he or she understand the nature of the opponent.

You should ensure you use a lawyer when you are faced with the dissemination of photographs and videos of a sexual nature. Such "revenge porn" cases are gaining in prominence and you stand more chance of securing an injunction to prevent their broadcast, the withdrawal of the publication and potential criminal sanctions. You will be able to obtain a variety of orders which leads to the delivery up of this material (even if in encrypted form), the prohibition on possession and broadcast and significant sanctions if these are breached. Your lawyer can also cause third parties to comply with these orders and obtain information from these third parties as to the originating parties. This is why we often use lieutenants with these matters but ultimately you will be able to counter something as serious as this. You should keep legal action for the most serious matters arising from smear campaigns.

h. Your energies should be applied to winning the battle concerning the audience (see points that follow) and not fighting us. You will not defeat us because we always change the battleground. I mentioned at the outset there are three parties to a smear campaign – a victim, the instigator and the audience. A smear won't work with an unreceptive audience. That is the battleground you need to target.

i. In terms of the audience forget those people who are Turncoats. You will not persuade them, they will report back to us and we gain fuel from your attempts. Forget these people. No matter if they are family, once were close friends and so on, they are not worth bothering with. If they have accepted what we have to say they will not change from this and you are only wasting precious and limited energy dealing with these people. We hope that you will do so as you become bogged down tackling enemies you cannot defeat. Pick your opponents in the audience battleground carefully. Forget the Turncoats. You will lose family and friends but that is the price that has to be paid. Did you want to be continue to engage with such people anyway?

j. Who do you need? Identify those people. If they are not Turncoats use your energy to get them onside. Do this without excessive emotion, without hyperbole and drama. Present the facts and if you have independent evidence use that to your advantage. Never tell the audience member what to think, people resent that. Let them reach their own conclusion. If you do that you will recruit someone who will prove an unshakeable ally in dealing with the smear campaign on your behalf. Pick the people who can provide you with assistance (a place to stay, money, emotional support, transport, child care etc.) and approach them as described above.

k. Only attempt to persuade these people once. If you keep going they will be irritated and will either not help you or worse turn against you. If you cannot persuade them leave them be. Hopefully they will not get involved and that is as far as their involvement goes. Save your energy for other prospective targets.

l. Always be prepared to cut your losses. We know you want everyone to know the truth but the sooner you accept that this cannot be achieved the greater your prospects of dealing with the smear campaign in a more effective fashion. When the smear campaign has been unleashed without you knowing you cannot achieve total victory, you cannot have the last word, understand this, withdraw, conserve your energy and apply it the areas where you can win, rather than fighting unwinnable skirmishes.

m. Use someone who is unknown to us. They will be untouched from the smear campaign and this person will prove to be a considerable ally.

n. Find new supporters. These people will be untainted by the smear campaign. Make new friends. Look to involve yourself with people who understand what has happened to you (there are plenty of online forums) as not only will this help you deal with the emotional fallout it will distract you.

o. If people come to you and make mention of the smear and ask you whether it is true, confirm it is not true and then laugh off the suggestion. Being light-hearted about the smear to a third party (even if you do not feel it) will show the third party that it is not affecting you and therefore they are more likely to believe it is not true. In addition, this reaction will most likely feed back to us and we will be annoyed with your reaction. How dare you laugh at our machinations?

p. Do not plaster social media with how you feel. We will be watching. Our lieutenants will be watching and this will provide us with fuel. This will tell us it is working and it will energise us to continue it.

q. Do not look at our social media. There is no point. You will not like what you see as by this stage, when you know about the smear, we will be rolling it out on social media. Our own real profiles will be used to highlight your reactions (rather than propound the smear) and this will make you react all the more when we point out how ridiculous you are etc.

r. You would be well advised to remove your social media profiles and if you require an online presence (e.g. for forums etc.) create new false one which we cannot find. Engage with like-minded people online by all means but do so from a position of anonymity.

s. Do not start a blog about your experiences. This is like writing a book about us and we will love the attention and reaction. This is massive fuel for us.

t. Instigate no contact if not already done so.

We want you to react to the smear. If you do not, this is a hammer blow against it. Cut loose those people who will not be persuaded. They will only upset you and use up precious energy. Some people can never be persuaded. Rather than look to correct the smear you need to look to your own defences, put those in place, recruit wisely those who can support you, find new supporters and you will then be able to ride out the smear campaign. You will benefit in two senses: -

1. You will feel less exposed to the smear with additional support;
2. The removal of its energy means its effects and duration will be reduced.

You may be able to neutralise the smear more quickly through reliance on trusted supporters. Use them to do this. They have more energy and they are more likely to be believed by other people, thus creating an antidote which counters the smear, rather than you emotionally harping on about it.

You will not change the mind of everyone. Those who cannot be persuaded must be dropped. You should liken it to chopping off a gangrenous foot to save your life. There will be damage but you can minimise it, reduce the effect of the smear campaign and by not engaging with us you will infuriate us also. The smear will not last forever because ultimately fresh prospects and targets will gain our attention. Like any fire, if you do not provide fuel it will die out and this is the approach you must adopt to counter a smear campaign.

Thus you now understand all about the narcissistic smear campaign and what you can do to counter the effects. Armed with this understanding you will be placed in a prime position to ride out the smear campaign. You may emerge with a few smudges on you but you will not be stained as you might once have been.

Further required reading from H G Tudor

Evil

Narcissist: Seduction

Narcissist: Ensnared

Manipulated

Confessions of a Narcissist

More Confessions of a Narcissist

Further Confessions of a Narcissist

From the Mouth of a Narcissist

Escape: How to Beat the Narcissist

Danger: 50 Things You Should Not Do with a Narcissist

Departure Imminent: Preparing for No Contact to beat the Narcissist

Fuel

Chained: The Narcissist's Co-Dependent

A Delinquent Mind

Fury

Beautiful and Barbaric

The Devil's Toolkit

Sex and the Narcissist

Treasured and Tormented

No Contact: How to Beat the Narcissist

Revenge: How to Beat the Narcissist

Adored and Abhorred

Sitting Target: How and Why the Narcissist Chooses You

Black Hole: The Narcissistic Hoover

A Grimoire of Narcissism

Cherished and Chastised

Red Flag: 50 Warning Signs of Narcissistic Seduction

Ask the Narcissist: The Answers to Your Questions

Darlings and Demons

Black Flag: 50 Warning Signs of Abuse

Your Fault: Blame and the Narcissist

Elated and Eroded

Outnumber Not Outgunned

Deciphered: What the Narcissist Really Means

Feted and Feared

All available on Amazon

Further interaction with H G Tudor

Knowing the Narcissist

@narcissist_me

Facebook

Narcsite.wordpress.com

Printed in Great Britain
by Amazon